The Executor & Trustee Guide to Estate Settlement

A Complete Guide to Estate or Trust Settlement with Strategies That Save Thousands in Legal Fees

Library of Congress Cataloging-in-Publication Data: TXu-2-480-053
ISBN: 979-8-9928224-2-7

Dedication to the Reader
Thank you for trusting this guide to assist you through the trustee process. It is shared with the hope of empowering you to navigate this complex journey with confidence and clarity.

"Empowerment begins with knowledge, and knowledge begins with the courage to seek it. In navigating the unknown, we find our strength."

~Unknown

Table of Contents

6. **Secure the Deceased's Assets**

- Identifying and taking inventory of assets
- Securing real estate, financial accounts, and personal property
- Handling assets not in the trust

7. **Notifying Beneficiaries**

- Writing and sending notification letters
- Handling disputes or questions
- Documenting all communications

8. **Notifying Creditors**

- Drafting and publishing a notice to creditors
- Sending direct notices to known creditors
- Handling claims and disputes

9. **Obtain a Tax ID for the Trust**

- Understanding revocable vs. irrevocable trusts
- How to apply for an EIN online or by mail
- Setting up a trust bank account

10. **Understanding Probate**

- What probate is and when it's required
- Filing the probate application and managing the process
- Simplified probate options and templates

11. Managing Real Estate

- Deciding whether to sell or retain property
- Addressing mortgages, taxes, and obligations
- Preparing real estate for sale

12. Distribute Remaining Assets

- Following the trust's instructions for distribution
- Handling vehicles, boats, and similar property
- Finalizing asset transfers and documentation

13. Close the Trust

- Preparing final accounting and obtaining releases
- Filing final tax returns
- Declaration of trust closure and checklist

14. Wrapping It All Up

- Reflection on the trustee journey
- Key takeaways and encouragement
- Resources for continued learning

Free Downloads to Help You Get Started

To make this process even easier, we've created a **free downloadable toolkit** with all the templates, checklists, and worksheets referenced in this book.

Access them here:
https://linktr.ee/YourExecutorAndTrusteeGuide

Includes:

- Legal notice templates

- Expense tracking spreadsheets

- Communication logs

- Final distribution forms

- The official **Estate Settlement Workbook**

These tools are designed to help you stay organized, compliant, and confident—every step of the way.

Chapter 1
Introduction

If you're reading this book, it means someone close to you—a loved one—has passed away, and you have been entrusted with a critical role: settling their estate.

First, let me extend my condolences. Losing a loved one is difficult enough, and being responsible for their estate can feel overwhelming.

If you have been named as the Executor in a Will and the Trustee of a Living Trust, you are now responsible for managing their assets, handling legal and financial matters, and ensuring their final wishes are carried out.

If you're like many people stepping into this role, you might be asking:

- What exactly am I supposed to do?
- Do I need an attorney, or can I handle this myself?
- How do I manage probate or trust administration without making costly mistakes?
- Is there a way to avoid excessive legal fees?

The answer is: Yes—you can do this, and this book will show you how.

This guide was created from personal experience—walking the same path you're now on.

I was handed the responsibility of managing a loved one's estate as not only the Trustee but also the Executor and quickly realized that estate attorneys charge thousands of dollars for tasks that, with the right knowledge, most people can do themselves.

My goal is to give you that knowledge in a clear, step-by-step format, so you can confidently settle the estate or trust while saving money on unnecessary legal fees.

Who Is This Book For?

This book is designed specifically for those who have been named as both an Executor and Trustee, providing comprehensive guidance on handling both roles.

However, if you are serving only as an Executor managing a Will through probate or solely as a Trustee administering a trust, this guide will still walk you through the necessary steps for your specific responsibilities—ensuring you navigate the process with clarity and confidence.

This guide will help you:

✔**Understand Your Legal Responsibilities** – Learn what an executor or trustee must do, when to take action, and how to avoid common pitfalls.

✔ **Navigate Probate or Trust Administration** – Get clear, actionable steps for both processes.

✔ **Handle Assets & Debts Properly** – Manage bank accounts, real estate, investments, and creditor claims.

✔ **Distribute Inheritances Correctly** – Follow the legal guidelines to avoid disputes among beneficiaries.

✔ **Minimize Costs & Save Money** – Avoid unnecessary attorney fees while ensuring everything is done legally and correctly.

If you have the means and prefer to hire an attorney, that's always an option. But if you're looking to save thousands of dollars and take control of the process, this book will empower you to do just that.
You don't need a law degree—you just need a roadmap. This book is that roadmap.

Let's get started.

Chapter 2
The Roadmap

Navigating the process of settling an estate or administering a trust can feel overwhelming. If you have been named both an **Executor,** responsible for managing probate, and a **Trustee,** handling trust administration, this guide will help you understand your role and responsibilities. Some readers may be tasked with one or the other, which requires handling distinct processes for different types of assets.

This chapter provides a **step-by-step roadmap** of the entire estate and trust settlement process, helping you stay organized and avoid unnecessary legal expenses.

Steps to Settle an Estate or Trust

Each of the following steps will be covered in detail in subsequent chapters. This overview gives you a high-level understanding of the process.

1. **Gather Essential Documents:**

     o   Collect the trust document, Will, death certificate, financial statements, and property deeds.

2. **Understand Your Role as Executor and Trustee & Consult an Estate Attorney:**

   ○ Review the trust document to understand your responsibilities, timelines, and the scope of your authority.

   ○ Find a reputable estate attorney for a consultation to ask critical questions and arm yourself with knowledge to handle the process independently.

   ○ **Tip:** Even if you plan to handle the process yourself, a one-time consultation with an estate attorney can save you thousands by providing guidance on what you can do independently.

3. **Create the Certificate of Trust in Existence and Authority or Obtain Letters Testamentary**

   ○ This critical document verifies the existence of the trust and the trustee's authority to act. It is often required by financial institutions, title companies, and other entities when managing or transferring trust assets.

4. **Secure the Deceased's Assets**:

   o   Take inventory of all assets, including real estate, bank accounts, retirement accounts, and personal property.

5. **Notify Beneficiaries**:

   o   Inform all beneficiaries and interested parties about the trust and their role in it.

6. **Notify Creditors**:

   o   Publish a notice to creditors in a local newspaper and send direct notices to known creditors. This is an essential step to identify and address any debts owed by the trust.

7. **Obtain a Tax ID for the Trust**:

   o   If the trust is now irrevocable, you'll need an Employer Identification Number (EIN) from the IRS.

8. **Understand Probate**:

   o   Learn what probate is, when it's necessary, and how to navigate the process, including filing the required documents and avoiding unnecessary expenses.

9. **Manage Real Estate**:

   o   Decide whether to sell or retain the property, and address any mortgages or tax issues.

9. **Settle Debts and Taxes**:

   o   Use trust assets to pay outstanding debts, medical bills, and taxes. This may include filing the decedent's final income tax return.

11. **Distribute Remaining Assets**:

   o   Follow the trust's instructions for distributing assets to beneficiaries.

12. **Close the Trust**:

   o   Once all tasks are completed, create a final accounting, distribute remaining funds, and formally close the trust.

Each of these steps involves specific tasks, documents, and potential pitfalls. The rest of the book will delve into each step in detail, providing you with all the tools and guidance you need.

Important Terms and Definitions

- **Trustee**: The person responsible for administering the trust according to its terms and applicable laws.

- **Beneficiary**: A person or entity entitled to receive assets or benefits from the trust.

- **Probate**: The legal process of administering a deceased person's estate.

- **Irrevocable Trust**: A trust that cannot be amended or revoked after the settlor's death.

- **Fiduciary Duty**: A trustee's legal obligation to act in the best interests of the beneficiaries.

- **Certificate of Trust in Existence and Authority**: A document that verifies the existence of the trust and the trustee's authority to act.

- **Letters Testamentary** – A legal document issued by the probate court authorizing the **Executor** of a Will to act on behalf of the deceased's estate. This document grants the

Executor the legal authority to manage assets, pay debts, and distribute property according to the Will's instructions.

More terms will be defined as needed throughout the book.

Documents You Will Need to Create or Obtain

Executor (Probate Administration)

1. **Will:**
   Serves as legal proof of the deceased's final wishes and inheritance instructions, guiding the probate process.

2. **Death Certificate:**
   Required to notify financial institutions, government agencies, and creditors of the deceased's passing.

3. **Letters Testamentary:**
   A court-issued document that grants the Executor legal authority to manage and distribute the estate.

4. **Probate Application & Court Forms:**
   Necessary paperwork to officially initiate the probate process and request the Executor's appointment.

5. **Notice to Creditors:**
A public notification in a local newspaper informing potential claimants about the estate settlement process.

6. **Final Accounting Forms:**
Detailed records of all probate transactions, asset distributions, and expenses, often required for court approval.

Trustee (Trust Administration)

1. **Trust Agreement:**
The governing document outlining the trust's terms, the trustee's responsibilities, and beneficiary distributions.

2. **Certificate of Trust in Existence and Authority:**
A document that verifies the trustee's legal authority to act on behalf of the trust without revealing the full trust details.

3. **Death Certificate:**
Required for financial institutions, government agencies, and asset transfers related to the trust administration.

4. **Tax ID Number (EIN):**
A unique identifier assigned by the IRS, necessary for trust

tax filings and financial transactions.

5.   **Final Accounting Documents:**
     A record of all trust transactions, income, expenses, and distributions, provided to beneficiaries for transparency.

An index at the end of this book will include templates for all these documents.

Who You Need to Hire

Did I retain an estate attorney to do the process for me? No. That would have cost me a $3,000 retainer and thousands more by the end of the process. Instead, I paid an estate attorney $500 for an hour-long consultation.

I sent them the Will and trust ahead of time for review and came to the meeting prepared with a list of questions that allowed me to navigate the process on my own.

I then used ChatGPT to create the templates for the necessary documents and hired a legal document preparer (LDA) to review and finalize the documents, ensuring they were state-compliant. This approach saved me a lot of money.

While this book is designed to help you **avoid unnecessary legal fees**, there are still instances where professional help can be valuable.

Here's who you need on your team:

1. **Estate Attorney**:

   ○ While you won't need to retain one for the entire process, a consultation can provide critical insights into understanding probate laws, and answer legal questions.

   ○ We will go into more detail about finding and utilizing an estate attorney in Chapter 4.

2. **Legal Document Preparer (LDA)**:

   ○ LDAs are professionals who specialize in preparing legal documents and can ensure your documents comply with state laws. This option is a cost-effective alternative to attorneys for preparing probate filings, trust documents, and creditor notices.

What Is a Legal Document Preparer (LDA)?

   ○ An LDA is a certified professional who prepares legal documents at your direction. Unlike attorneys, they do not provide legal advice but assist with document creation for a fraction of the cost.

Difference Between LDA and Paralegal:

- ○ Paralegals work under the supervision of an attorney and cannot work independently, while LDAs are authorized to work directly with clients without attorney oversight.

3. **CPA or Tax Professional:** If the estate or trust has income-producing assets, you may need assistance filing estate or trust tax returns (Form 1041).

4. **Real Estate Agent:** If property needs to be sold, a licensed agent familiar with estate transactions can simplify the process.

My Experience

When I needed a legal document, I combined both approaches. I had ChatGPT create the document by uploading the trust and Will, then hired an LDA to review it and ensure compliance with state laws. The LDA also filed the document for me.

This approach saved me a significant amount of money. An attorney quoted me a $1,300 retainer, with additional fees, while the LDA charged me only $150.

Executor vs. Trustee: What's the Difference?

Role	Executor (Handles Probate Estate)	Trustee (Manages a Trust)
Legal Authority	Appointed by the court via **Letters Testamentary**	Named in the trust document, does **not** require court approval
Asset Control	Manages probate assets (anything not in a trust)	Controls trust assets directly, bypassing probate
Process	Must file for probate, notify heirs, and settle debts through court oversight	Administers the trust privately without court involvement
Debt Payment	Pays debts from the probate estate	Pays debts from trust funds
Distribution of Assets	Distributes assets **after probate is complete**	Follows trust instructions and distributes assets **immediately or as directed**

Key Takeaways

- If you are an **Executor**, your primary duty is to handle probate, settle debts, and distribute assets per the **Will**.

- If you are a **Trustee**, you will manage assets **already in a trust** and distribute them as outlined in the trust agreement **without probate**.

- If you are **both**, you must **separate probate duties from trust administration** and ensure compliance with both legal processes.

- By **following this roadmap**, you will be equipped to **settle an estate or trust efficiently, avoid unnecessary legal fees, and fulfill your loved one's wishes properly**.

By assembling the right team and using these cost-effective resources, you can confidently navigate the trustee process without overspending.

This chapter sets the stage for everything that follows. In the next section, we will dive deeper into **gathering the essential documents needed to begin estate and trust administration.**

Chapter 3
Gathering Essential Documents

One of the first and most critical tasks in settling an estate or administering a trust is gathering the necessary documents.

Whether you are serving as an **Executor**, a **Trustee**, or both, having all relevant paperwork in order will ensure a smooth and efficient process. These documents will help you access financial accounts, transfer property, notify creditors, and meet legal obligations.

This chapter will walk you through the documents you need, where to find them, and how to keep them organized.

Essential Documents Checklist

Depending on whether you are handling a **probate estate** or a **trust**, you will need some or all of the following documents:

Executor (Probate Administration)

- **Will** – Establishes the decedent's final wishes for asset distribution.

- **Death Certificate** – Required by financial institutions, government agencies, and courts.

- **Letters Testamentary** – Court-issued document granting the executor legal authority to act on behalf of the estate.

- **Probate Court Forms** – Required to open and process probate (varies by state).

- **Notice to Creditors** – A public notification for potential claims against the estate.

- **Final Accounting Forms** – Documentation of the estate's financial transactions.

Trustee (Trust Administration)

- **Trust Agreement** – The legal document that outlines how the trust assets should be managed and distributed.

- **Certificate of Trust** – A condensed version of the trust document that proves your authority without disclosing full details.

- **Death Certificate** – Needed for financial institutions and legal transfers.

- **EIN (Employer Identification Number)** – Required if the trust is now irrevocable.

- **Final Accounting Documents** – Records of all financial transactions to share with beneficiaries.

Keeping these documents well-organized from the start will help streamline the administration process and avoid delays.

1. The Original Will

- **Why It's Needed**: The original Will is often required to prove the decedent's wishes, especially if probate is involved.

- **How to Obtain It**: The original Will is typically stored with the decedent's important documents, a safety deposit box, or their attorney.

- **What If It's Missing**: If you cannot locate the original, consult with an estate attorney immediately to understand your options.

2. Death Certificate

Why It's Needed: An original death certificate is required for financial institutions, government agencies, and creditors.

How to Obtain It:

- Contact the funeral home or mortuary that handled the arrangements.

- Request multiple certified copies (usually 6-10).

- You can also obtain the death certificate from the **county vital records office** where the individual passed away.

Finding the Vital Records Office: Search online using terms like "Vital Records Office [County Name]" or "Death Certificate [County Name]."

- **Required Documents**: You'll need:

    o   A valid photo ID.

    o   Proof of your relationship to the deceased or legal authority as trustee (e.g., trust document, notarized statement).

    o   The decedent's full name, date of death, and Social Security number.

If a prior trustee has passed, you'll need their death certificate as well. Request this through the county vital records office where they died.

Special Note for Non-Immediate Family Members: If you are not an immediate family member, you may need to provide additional proof of your legal authority, such as a notarized copy of the trust or a court order appointing you as trustee.

3. Trust Documents

Why They're Needed: The trust document outlines your authority and responsibilities.

Where to Find It:

- With the deceased's important papers.

- In an attorney's office.

- In a safe deposit box or digital storage.

What If It's Missing? If you cannot locate the trust document, check with family members, financial institutions, or attorneys who may have worked with the deceased.

How to Organize Them: Make copies and keep the original in a safe place. Also scan the trust, will, and death certificates and keep a folder on your computer of. You will need to email these often.

4. Financial Statements

Types to Gather: Bank accounts, investment portfolios, retirement accounts, and life insurance policies.

How to Obtain Them: Contact financial institutions with proof of authority (death certificate, trust document. Although some will require a Certificate of Trust in Existence and Authority.). You may also be able to find these in files in their home.

How to Request Statements:

- o Contact the financial institution with a certified death certificate and you're executor/trustee authorization.

- o Some institutions may require a **Certificate of Trust** or **Letters Testamentary**.

5. Credit Report

Why It's Needed: A credit report helps identify outstanding debts or unknown creditors.

How to Obtain It:

Send a written request to the three major credit bureaus:

- **Equifax**: P.O. Box 105139, Atlanta, GA 30348-5139.

- **Experian**: P.O. Box 9701, Allen, TX 75013.

- **TransUnion**: P.O. Box 2000, Chester, PA 19016-2000.

Include the decedent's name, Social Security number, date of birth, death certificate, and proof of your authority as trustee.

6. Deeds and Titles

Why They're Needed: These documents are essential for managing real estate and vehicles.

Where to Find It:

- Deeds: County recorder's office, attorney's office, or personal files.

- Vehicle Titles: State DMV, personal files, or trust documents.

What If It's Missing?

- o Request a certified copy of the deed from the county recorder's office.

- o Apply for a duplicate vehicle title through the DMV.

7. Other Pertinent Records

- Tax returns for the past three years.

- Safe deposit box inventory.

- Employment records (for final paychecks or benefits).

8. If You're a Trustee and Beneficiary

Relinquishing Trustee Role: You can step down as trustee and appoint a successor while still remaining a beneficiary. Or remain both. This means as the Trustee you will be doing all the work necessary to deal with all the assets and disburse them amongst the beneficiaries.

How It Works: Sign a resignation document and file it as required. You can create this document yourself using the template below, or you can:

o Copy and paste the template into ChatGPT and upload the trust and will for review. ChatGPT can help generate a tailored resignation document based on your input. Be sure to review the final document yourself to confirm it's accurate.

o **Hire a Legal Document Preparer (LDA)**: LDAs are professionals who specialize in preparing legal documents and can ensure your resignation document complies with state laws. This option is significantly less expensive than hiring an attorney.

We've included a Trustee Resignation Form Template on the following page.

Resignation Document Template

Trustee Resignation Form

State of [State]
County of [County]

Re: The [Name of Trust]

I, [Your Full Name], the undersigned, hereby resign as Trustee of The [Name of Trust], dated [Date of Trust]. My resignation is effective as of [Date].

I certify that I have provided written notice of my resignation to the following parties:

- [Successor Trustee's Full Name]

- [Beneficiaries]

I hereby transfer all authority, duties, and responsibilities of the Trustee to [Successor Trustee's Full Name], as outlined in the trust document.

Dated: [Date]

Signed:
[Your Full Name]

Acknowledgment

State of [State]
County of [County]

On this [Date] day of [Month], [Year], before me, [Notary Public's Name], personally appeared [Your Full Name], known to me (or proved to me on the basis of satisfactory evidence) to be the person whose name is subscribed to this instrument and acknowledged to me that he/she executed it in their authorized capacity.

Witness my hand and official seal:

[Notary Public's Signature]
[Notary Public's Name]
My Commission Expires: [Expiration Date]

If you are using ChatGPT to create this document, copy and paste the following prompt:

"Using the template below, create a Trustee Resignation Form for me. I will upload my trust and Will documents for reference. Please include all necessary details, such as the trust's name, date of execution, settlor(s), my name as the resigning trustee, and the successor trustee's name. Ensure it complies with general state requirements and is ready for notarization."

By gathering these documents promptly and thoroughly, you'll set yourself up for success in administering the trust. Let's move forward with understanding your role in more detail.

Organizing Your Documents

Once you have gathered the necessary documents, keep them organized to ensure quick access throughout the estate or trust administration process.

Suggested Organization Method:

1.   **Create Digital Copies:** Scan all documents and save them in a secure cloud folder.

2.   **Use a Filing System:** Keep originals in a labeled binder or locked fireproof box.

3. **Track Everything:** Use a spreadsheet to log document locations and access dates.

4. **Secure Access:** Limit access to these documents to authorized individuals (e.g., co-trustees, estate attorney).

Key Takeaways

- **Executors** need to collect probate documents, including the **Will, Letters Testamentary, and Notice to Creditors**.

- **Trustees** require the **Trust Agreement, Certificate of Trust, and EIN** for administration.

- Death certificates, financial statements, and property records are essential for both roles.

- Keeping documents well-organized from the start will make the estate or trust settlement process much smoother.

With your essential documents gathered, you are now ready to take the next step: **understanding your legal responsibilities and determining whether probate is required**. The following chapter will guide you through this process in detail.

Chapter 4
Understand Your Role as Executor or Trustee & Consulting an Estate Attorney

Taking on the role of Executor or Trustee is a significant legal responsibility. These roles require you to act in the best interest of beneficiaries, follow legal procedures, and ensure that the deceased's wishes are properly carried out.

To navigate the process effectively, you need to fully understand your duties, timelines, and the scope of your authority.

This chapter will help you understand your specific duties, the differences between the roles, and how to prepare for your responsibilities effectively.

It will guide you through reviewing the trust document, and show you how to make the most of a consultation with an estate attorney to save money while ensuring you're equipped to handle the process.

Topics will include:

- The difference between an executor and trustee.

- A step-by-step guide to assuming your role as both an executor and trustee.

- Tips for finding a reputable estate attorney

- Critical questions to ask during the consultation

- How to use the consultation to gather all necessary information for independent administration.

Executor vs. Trustee: What's the Difference?

Both Executors and Trustees oversee the transfer of assets, but they operate under different legal frameworks. Here's a breakdown of their key differences:

Role	Executor (Probate Estate)	Trustee (Trust Administration)
Legal Authority	Appointed by the probate court through **Letters Testamentary**	Named in the trust document, no court involvement required
Asset Control	Manages probate assets (anything not in a trust)	Controls trust assets directly, bypassing probate
Process	Files for probate, notifies heirs, settles debts through court oversight	Administers the trust privately following its terms
Debt Payment	Pays debts using probate estate funds	Pays debts using trust funds
Asset Distribution	Distributes assets after probate completion	Distributes assets as directed by the trust

If you are serving as **both Executor and Trustee**, you must manage **two separate processes**—one for probate assets and another for trust assets.

38

Fiduciary Duty: Your Legal Obligation

Both Executors and Trustees have a **fiduciary duty**, which means you are legally required to act in the best interests of the estate or trust beneficiaries. This includes:

- **Acting in Good Faith:** Making decisions based on fairness and the wishes of the deceased and with loyalty to the beneficiaries, always prioritize their interests over your own.

- **Avoiding Conflicts of Interest:** You cannot personally benefit from estate or trust assets unless specified. All decisions must be made to benefit the beneficiaries, even if they conflict with your personal interests.

- **Maintaining Transparency:** Keeping clear records and providing beneficiaries with necessary information including major actions, such as selling assets or distributing funds.

- **Following Legal Requirements:** Ensuring proper handling of all financial, tax, and legal matters such as borrowing trust funds or engaging in transactions where you personally benefit.

Failing to meet these responsibilities can result in legal consequences, including removal from your position or personal financial liability.

Steps to Fulfill This Duty:

- ○ Regularly communicate with beneficiaries about trust activities.

- ○ Document all decisions and the rationale behind them.

- ○ Seek legal or professional advice if a conflict of interest arises.

Steps to Prepare for Your Role

Below is an overview of the key steps you will need to take as both an executor and trustee.

Step 1: Review the Will or Trust Document

- **Executors**: Identify key provisions, including named beneficiaries and probate instructions.

- **Trustees**: Understand the trust's terms, including any specific asset management or distribution guidelines.

- **Check for Special Instructions**: Some documents contain provisions for minor children, charitable donations, or specific asset handling.

Step2: Identify Assets & Liabilities

- Gather an inventory of assets, including **bank accounts, real estate, investments, vehicles, and personal property**.

- Determine **debts and liabilities**, including mortgages, credit card debt, medical bills, and loans.

- Executors must verify which assets require **probate** and which can be transferred without it.

Step 3: Notify Beneficiaries & Interested Parties

- **Executors:** Send formal notices to heirs named in the Will and those legally entitled to inheritance.

- **Trustees:** Notify beneficiaries of their rights under the trust.

- **Transparency is Key**: Keeping beneficiaries informed reduces disputes and legal challenges.

Step 4: Asset Management:

Steps to Secure Assets: Both Executors and Trustees are responsible for securing assets, though the steps differ based on their roles:

1. **Create an inventory of all known assets:**

    - List real estate, bank accounts, investment portfolios, retirement accounts, personal property, and debts.

2. **Notify financial institutions:**

    - Provide required documentation (Letters Testamentary for Executors, Certificate of Trust for Trustees).

    - Retitle or consolidate accounts as needed.

3. **Hire professionals as needed:**

    - Work with appraisers, real estate agents, accountants, or attorneys to assess and manage assets.

Here are detail for each type of asset:

Bank Accounts

- Open a new bank account in the name of the trust or estate to manage all financial transactions. This account will be used to deposit proceeds from real estate sales, collect income, and pay expenses.

- Transfer financial assets, such as cash from the decedent's accounts, into the new account to consolidate management.

- Alternatively, ensure existing accounts are retitled in the trust's name if consolidation is not feasible.

Executors: Open an estate account to manage probate-related transactions.

Trustees: If required, open a separate trust account for ongoing management.

*Never mix estate or trust funds with personal accounts.

Real Estate

Executors and Trustees must take steps to secure and manage real estate assets responsibly.

If you are an Executor:

- o Retitle property deeds to reflect estate ownership if required by probate.

- o Secure real estate by changing locks, keeping utilities current, and ensuring adequate insurance coverage.

- o Work with the probate court to determine how and when the property can be sold or transferred unless the property is in the trust.

- o Consult a real estate agent or appraiser to establish the property's market value.

If you are a Trustee:

- o Retitle property deeds to reflect trust ownership, if not already done.

- o Secure real estate by changing locks, keeping utilities current, and ensuring adequate insurance coverage.

- o Follow the trust's instructions regarding retaining, managing, or selling the property.

- o Work with real estate professionals to assess and manage property transactions.

Life Insurance Policies

Executors and Trustees may need to handle life insurance policies, depending on the named beneficiaries:

If the trust or estate is the beneficiary:

File a claim with the insurance company. You will need:
- A certified copy of the death certificate.
- The policy number or documentation.
- Proof of your authority as **Executor** (Letters Testamentary) or **Trustee** (Certificate of Trust).

Next:

  o Contact the insurance company for specific instructions and required forms.

  o Ensure that any proceeds received are managed and distributed according to the terms of the Will or trust.

If an individual beneficiary is named:

  o The beneficiary should file the claim directly.

  o The proceeds do not go through probate or trust administration unless otherwise specified.

Investments

Executors and Trustees must assess and manage investment assets appropriately:

If you are an Executor:

  o Identify and secure all investment accounts.

  o Determine if investments need to be liquidated to pay estate expenses.

  o Consult a financial advisor or estate attorney for guidance on required actions.

- o Transfer investments to beneficiaries in accordance with the Will and court approval.

If you are a Trustee:

- o Review existing investments to ensure they align with the trust's goals.

- o Work with a financial advisor if necessary to make informed investment decisions.

- o Distribute investments to beneficiaries as outlined in the trust agreement.

Step 5: Debt and Expense Payment

Executors and Trustees must ensure all valid debts and expenses are properly settled:

If you are an Executor:

- o Use estate funds to settle debts, including:
  - Final medical bills.
  - Funeral expenses.
  - Probate and legal fees.

- Notify creditors and allow them time to submit claims as required by probate law.

- Ensure debts are paid in the correct legal order before distributing assets to heirs.

If you are a Trustee:

Use trust funds to settle debts assigned to the trust, including:

- Trust administration costs.
- Any debts for which the trust is legally responsible.

*Ensure that all financial obligations are resolved before distributing assets to beneficiaries.

Steps to Pay Debts

1. **Identify all known creditors and notify them** (as required by law).

2. **Verify the validity of each claim** before making payments.

3. **Use estate or trust funds** to settle valid claims in priority order.

4. **Maintain detailed records** of all payments made for final accounting.

Step 6: Record-Keeping

Maintaining detailed records is essential for both **Executors** and **Trustees** to protect themselves and fulfill their legal responsibilities.

Executors must track:

- Probate filings and court orders.
- Payments made to creditors and administrative expenses.
- Asset sales and distributions to heirs.

Trustees must track:

- Trust-related income, expenses, and distributions.
- Communications with beneficiaries and third parties.
- Investment management and trust bank account transactions.

Why It's Important:

- Beneficiaries have the right to request an accounting of estate or trust activities.

- Clear records help prevent or resolve disputes.

- Proper documentation protects the Executor or Trustee from legal liability.

How to Do It:

- Use a spreadsheet, accounting software, or a professional bookkeeper.

- Keep both physical and digital records of all transactions.

Step 7: Distribute Assets

Distributing assets depends on whether the administration is under probate or a trust:

If you are an Executor:

- Obtain court approval if required before distributing assets.

- Follow the Will's instructions for who receives what.

o Transfer titles, real estate, and financial accounts to heirs accordingly.

If you are a Trustee:

o Follow the trust's distribution instructions.

o Transfer assets directly to beneficiaries without court involvement.

o Ensure all debts and taxes are settled before making distributions.

Steps to Distribute Assets

1. **Verify that all obligations have been met** (debts, taxes, and expenses).

2. **Prepare a final accounting** and share it with beneficiaries if required.

3. **Obtain signed receipts from beneficiaries** upon asset distribution.

Step 8: Legal and Tax Compliance

Both Executors and Trustees have tax and legal obligations. The estate or trust may owe income taxes, property taxes, or estate taxes.

Consult a CPA or tax professional to determine what filings are required. Executors may need to file the decedent's **final income tax return**.

If you are an Executor:

- o   File the decedent's final income tax return.
- o   File the estate's tax return if necessary.
- o   Ensure compliance with probate court requirements.

If you are a Trustee:

- o   File tax returns for the trust if it generates income.
- o   Ensure distributions are handled in accordance with tax laws.

Steps to Ensure Compliance:

1. Hire a CPA or tax professional to handle estate or trust tax filings.

2. Review state laws or consult an attorney to ensure proper filings.

Scope of Authority

Your authority as an **Executor** or **Trustee** is defined by the Will, trust document, and applicable state laws.

What You Can Do:
✔ **Executors:** Manage probate assets, pay estate debts, and distribute assets per the Will.

✔ **Trustees:** Manage trust assets, make distributions, and follow the trust's terms.

✔ **Both:** Open and manage estate or trust bank accounts, hire professionals, and oversee asset transfers.

What You Cannot Do:

✘ Use estate or trust assets for personal benefit (unless explicitly stated).

✘ Deviate from the terms of the Will or trust without proper authorization.

Decide Whether to Hire Professionals

While this guide aims to help you avoid unnecessary legal fees, professional assistance may still be necessary.

- **Estate Attorney:** Helps with probate filings, trust interpretation, and legal disputes.

- **Legal Document Preparer (LDP):** A cost-effective alternative for handling paperwork.

- **CPA or Tax Professional:** Ensures compliance with tax laws and reporting.

- **Real Estate Agent:** If property needs to be sold, a licensed agent familiar with estate sales can streamline the process.

Common Executor & Trustee Mistakes to Avoid

1. **Failing to Notify Creditors Properly**

   o   Executors must **publish a Notice to Creditors** in a local newspaper.

   o   Trustees must notify known creditors directly.

2. **Mismanaging Estate or Trust Funds**

   o   Always keep financial transactions **separate** from personal finances.

   o   Maintain **detailed records** of all income, expenses, and distributions.

3. **Distributing Assets Too Soon**

   o   **Do not distribute assets** until all debts, taxes, and expenses are resolved.

   o   Early distribution could result in **personal liability** for unpaid claims.

4. **Ignoring Beneficiaries' Rights**

    ○   Beneficiaries have a legal right to **information and fair treatment**.

    ○   Provide **regular updates** to maintain transparency.

5. **Neglecting Tax Filings**

    ○   Ensure estate or trust tax returns are filed correctly to avoid penalties.

Key Takeaways

- **Executors handle probate assets**, while **Trustees manage trust assets**.

- **Your fiduciary duty requires transparency, fairness, and compliance with the law**.

- **Following a structured process ensures smooth estate or trust administration**.

- **Seek professional guidance when needed to avoid costly mistakes**.

By understanding your role and responsibilities upfront, you can confidently navigate the estate or trust settlement process while minimizing unnecessary legal expenses.

In the next chapter, we'll cover **how to create the necessary legal documents to formalize your authority and begin asset management.**

Worksheet: Extracting Key Information from the Trust and Will

Use this worksheet to document the most important details from the **trust and/or Will**. Fill in the blanks as you review the documents.

General Information

For Executors (Will-Based Estate):

Decedent's Full Name: _____

Date of Death: _____

Date of Will Execution: _____

Executor(s) Named in Will: _____

Alternate Executor(s): _____

Court Jurisdiction (Probate Court): _____

For Trustees (Trust-Based Estate):

- Trust Name: _____
- Date of Trust Creation: _____
- Name of Settlor(s) (Trust Creator): _____
- Current Trustee(s): _____
- Successor Trustee(s): _____
- Irrevocable or Revocable? _____

Beneficiaries

For Both Executors and Trustees:

Primary Beneficiaries (Heirs/Trust Beneficiaries): _____

Contingent Beneficiaries (Backup Heirs/Beneficiaries): _____

Special Instructions for Beneficiaries: _____

Assets

List any assets that belong to the estate (for Executors) or the trust (for Trustees): _____

Real Estate (Include address and ownership details):

_____

Bank Accounts (Include financial institution and account type):

_____

Investment Accounts (Stocks, Bonds, Retirement Accounts, etc.):

_____

Personal Property (Jewelry, Vehicles, Collectibles, etc.):

_____

Business Interests (If applicable):

_____

Instructions & Distribution Details

For Executors (Probate Administration):

Specific Distribution Instructions in the Will: _____

Probate Required? (Yes/No) _____

Assets Subject to Probate: _____

Debts to Be Paid: _____

Taxes to Be Paid: _____

For Trustees (Trust Administration):

Trust Distribution Instructions: _____

Ongoing Trust or Lump-Sum Distribution? _____

Trust-Specific Debts (If applicable): _____

Tax Obligations for the Trust: _____

Legal & Administrative Requirements

For Executors (Probate Administration):

Letters Testamentary Required? (Yes/No) _____

Court Filing Deadlines: _____

Required Probate Forms (e.g., Petition for Probate): _____

For Trustees (Trust Administration):

Certificate of Trust Needed? (Yes/No) _____

Successor Trustee Appointment Needed? (Yes/No) _____

Steps for Asset Retitling or Transfer: _____

Final Notes & Action Items

Use this section to outline any outstanding tasks, deadlines, or special instructions:

Importance of Consulting an Estate Attorney

Even if you plan to handle the trustee process yourself, consulting with an estate attorney can provide essential insights and save you from costly mistakes. Here's why:

- **Understanding Complex Terms**: The attorney can clarify legal jargon and ensure you understand the trust document.

- **Identifying Risks**: They can point out potential legal or financial risks and how to address them.

- **State Law Guidance**: Trust laws vary by state, and an attorney can ensure compliance.

Cost Comparison

- Retaining an attorney for the entire process can cost $3,000-$10,000 or more.

- A one-hour consultation typically costs $250-$500.

How to Choose a Good Estate Attorney

When selecting an attorney for your consultation, consider these factors:

1. **Specialization**:

   ○ Choose someone who specializes in estate planning or probate law.

2. **Reputation**:

   ○ Read reviews and ask for recommendations.

- ○ Verify their credentials and state bar membership.

3. **Price**:

   - ○ Expect to pay $250-$500 for an hour-long consultation.

4. **Availability**:

   - ○ Choose an attorney who can meet within your desired timeline.

   - ○ Balance their reputation, price, and availability.

Questions to Ask During the Consultation

Consulting with an estate attorney is a critical step in ensuring you fully understand your responsibilities and avoid costly mistakes.

To make the most of your consultation, come prepared with a list of questions. Below are key questions divided into sections based on whether you are serving as an **Executor** (for a Will and probate administration) or a **Trustee** (for trust administration).

Here are some comprehensive questions to guide your discussion:

For Executors (Probate Administration):

1. Understanding My Role:

- What are my legal duties as the Executor?
- What are the first steps I need to take after being named Executor?
- What deadlines do I need to be aware of in the probate process?
- Am I personally liable for any debts or mistakes in the administration?

2. Probate Process & Court Requirements:

- Is probate required for this estate?
- How long does the probate process typically take in this state?
- What documents do I need to file with the probate court?
- What fees and costs should I expect throughout probate?

3. Managing Estate Assets & Debts:

- How do I locate and secure the decedent's assets?
- What accounts should I use to pay estate expenses?
- Can I sell real estate or other assets before probate is complete?

- What's the proper way to handle vehicles, personal property, or business interests?
- How do I address outstanding debts and handle creditor claims?
- **Do I qualify for a step-up in basis when selling the property?**

Definition of Step-Up in Basis: A step-up in basis is a tax provision that adjusts the value of an inherited asset (such as real estate) to its fair market value at the time of the decedent's death.

This means that if you sell the property, the capital gains tax is based only on the appreciation in value from the date of death, not the original purchase price.

Understanding whether the property qualifies for a step-up in basis can significantly reduce the tax burden on the trust or beneficiaries.

4. **Handling Beneficiaries & Distributions:**

- What's the correct process for notifying heirs and beneficiaries?
- What happens if a beneficiary contests the Will?
- Do I have discretion in how and when assets are distributed?

5. **Taxes & Finalizing the Estate:**

- o   What taxes need to be filed for the deceased and the estate?
- o   Do I need an Employer Identification Number (EIN) for the estate?
- o   What are the steps to close the estate after distributions are made?

6. **Legal Risks & Liability Protection:**

- o   How can I protect myself from potential lawsuits by creditors or beneficiaries?
- o   What happens if I make a mistake during probate?
- o   Should I consider Errors & Omissions insurance for Executors?

For Trustees (Trust Administration):

1. **Understanding My Role:**

- o   What are my fiduciary duties as a Trustee?
- o   How do I formally assume my role as Trustee?
- o   Am I personally liable for trust administration errors?

2. Managing Trust Assets:

- How do I retitle assets in the name of the trust?
- Do I need to consolidate financial accounts or keep them separate?
- How do I secure real estate and other physical trust assets?

3. Notifying Beneficiaries & Handling Disputes:

- What is my obligation to inform beneficiaries about the trust administration?
- How do I handle beneficiaries who dispute the terms of the trust?
- Am I required to provide beneficiaries with financial records?

4. Trust Distributions & Financial Management:

- What are the guidelines for distributing assets to beneficiaries?
- Can I sell trust assets if needed?
- How do I handle ongoing distributions for minor or disabled beneficiaries?

5. **Tax & Compliance Issues:**

  ○ Do I need to file taxes for the trust, and what forms should I use?

  ○ How do I obtain an EIN for the trust?

  ○ What are the tax implications of selling trust assets?

6. **Closing the Trust:**

  ○ What steps do I need to take before I can close the trust?

  ○ What kind of final accounting do I need to provide?

  ○ Do I need beneficiary approval before finalizing trust distributions?

For Both Executors and Trustees:

Regardless of your role, these additional questions can help clarify your responsibilities:

• Are there any state-specific laws I need to be aware of?

• What's the best way to document my actions to protect myself legally?

• How much flexibility do I have in managing assets and distributions?

- When should I hire professionals (e.g., CPAs, appraisers, financial advisors)?
- What are the best practices for keeping records and tracking expenses?

By preparing thoroughly and asking the right questions, you can gather the knowledge needed to confidently navigate the trustee process and minimize costs.

My Experience

When I took on the trustee role, I scheduled a one-hour consultation with an estate attorney. I sent them the Will and trust ahead of time for review and prepared a detailed list of questions.

This approach provided me with the knowledge I needed to proceed on my own, saving thousands of dollars.

The consultation cost $500, compared to the $3,000 retainer plus additional expensed and hourly rates I would have paid to retain the attorney for the entire process.

By combining this consultation with the use of ChatGPT for document templates and a Legal Document Preparer (LDA) for final reviews, I was able to complete the process efficiently and cost-effectively.

In the next chapter, we'll discuss securing and managing the deceased's assets.

Chapter 5

Create the Certificate of Trust in Existence and Authority and Letters Testamentary

One of the most important documents a **Trustee** needs when managing a trust is the **Certificate of Trust in Existence and Authority**. This document serves as legal proof of the trust's existence and the Trustee's authority to act on behalf of the trust.

If you are also serving as the **Executor**, you may not need this document for probate, but if the decedent had a trust, you will still need to create it to manage trust-held assets. Many financial institutions and title companies require this document before allowing transactions involving the trust.

Those serving as Executor may also need a **Letters Testamentary** document which is required in many estate administrations but **not always necessary**.

In essence, Letters Testamentary, is **proof of the Executor's authority**, similar to how a **Certificate of Trust** functions for Trustees. Financial institutions, government agencies, and other entities often require **Letters Testamentary** before allowing the Executor to handle the deceased's assets.

This chapter explains the purpose of the Certificate of Trust, when and where you need it, and how to create one.

What Is the Certificate of Trust in Existence and Authority?

A **Certificate of Trust** is a summary of the trust that provides key information without disclosing the full trust document. This allows you to confirm your authority without revealing all private details to banks, title companies, or other institutions.

It is often required by:

- **Financial Institutions**: To access or transfer accounts and investments held in the trust's name.

- **Title Companies**: For real estate transactions such as sales, transfers, or refinancing.

- **Other Entities**: Any organization or individual needing proof of your authority as trustee.

The certificate ensures privacy by summarizing essential information without disclosing sensitive details from the full trust document.

A **properly drafted Certificate of Trust** includes the following:

- The official **name of the trust**

- The **date** the trust was executed

- The **name(s) of the settlor(s)** (the person(s) who created the trust)

- The **name(s) of the current trustee(s)**

- A statement confirming that the trustee(s) has authority to act on behalf of the trust

- Whether the trust is **revocable or irrevocable**

- A declaration that the trust remains in effect and has not been revoked or modified in a way that affects its authority

Why Is It Important?

The Certificate of Trust is crucial for:

- **Confirming the Trust's Existence**: It verifies that the trust is valid and legally enforceable.

- **Proving Your Authority**: It demonstrates your legal power to act as trustee.

- **Facilitating Transactions**: Financial institutions, title companies, and others require this document to manage trust assets or conduct transactions.

What Will You Use It For?

A **Certificate of Trust** is necessary when dealing with:

- **Financial Institutions** – Banks and investment firms may require this document to confirm that the trustee has authority to manage trust-held accounts.

- **Real Estate Transactions** – If the trust owns real estate, a Certificate of Trust is often required for sales, refinancing, or title transfers.

- **Business Transactions** – If the trust holds shares in a business or other significant assets, third parties may require this document before proceeding with transactions.

- **Legal and Tax Filings** – Some government agencies and tax authorities may request this document when handling trust-related matters.

Without a Certificate of Trust, you may have to provide the entire trust document, which could contain sensitive information that beneficiaries or institutions do not need to see.

Steps to Create the Certificate of Trust

Follow these steps to prepare the Certificate of Trust in Existence and Authority:

Step 1: Review the Trust Document

Before drafting the certificate, locate the original **Trust Agreement** and verify:

- The official **trust name** and **date of execution**

- The **names of the settlor(s)** (the person(s) who created the trust)

- The **trustee(s) and successor trustee(s)**

- Whether the trust is **revocable or irrevocable**

- Any **specific powers** granted to the trustee

Ensure there are no clauses limiting your ability to act as trustee or obtain such a certificate.

Step 2: Verify the Will

- Check the Will for any references to the trust.

- Ensure it complements the trust's terms and addresses assets outside the trust that may require administration.

Step 3: Draft the Certificate of Trust

A Certificate of Trust typically includes:

- The name of the trust.

- The date the trust was executed.

- The names of the settlor(s) and trustee(s).

- A statement declaring whether the trust is revocable or irrevocable.

- Confirmation of the trustee's authority.

- A declaration that the trust has not been revoked, modified, or amended in a way that invalidates the certificate.

Step 4: Notarize the Certificate

Most banks, title companies, and financial institutions require the **Certificate of Trust** to be notarized. Locate a **notary public** at a:

- Local bank

- Courthouse

- Legal office

- Private notary service

Step 5: File or Provide the Certificate

Once notarized, you can submit copies to:

- Banks to manage trust accounts

- Title companies for real estate transactions

- Investment firms handling trust assets

- Any entity requesting proof of your authority as trustee

- For real estate transactions, confirm whether the certificate needs to be recorded with the county recorder's office or equivalent office in your jurisdiction.

Recording means officially filing the document with the local government office responsible for maintaining public records (often the county recorder or clerk's office).

 This step ensures the certificate becomes part of the public record, providing notice to third parties of the trustee's authority.

To record the document:

- Contact the county recorder's office to confirm requirements and fees.

- Bring or mail the notarized certificate along with any required forms or fees.

- Retain a certified copy of the recorded document for your records.

- Alternatively, a Legal Document Preparer (LDP) can handle the recording process for you for a small fee, ensuring compliance and saving you time. This is an excellent option if you prefer professional assistance.

Practical Advice

- **Contact Relevant Institutions**: Check with financial institutions, title companies, or other entities to confirm their specific requirements.

- **Be proactive.** Many institutions require a Certificate of Trust before processing transactions, so prepare it early.

- **Record if Necessary**: For real estate transactions, verify with the title company whether recording the certificate is needed.

- **Retain Copies**: Keep a notarized copy for presentation as required.

- **Confirm requirements.** Different institutions may have specific wording requirements—always check before submitting.

- **Consider professional review.** If unsure, an estate attorney or **Legal Document Preparer (LDP)** can ensure compliance with state laws.

By following these steps, you will have a legally compliant **Certificate of Trust in Existence and Authority** ready for use in managing trust affairs efficiently and professionally.

My Experience

When I needed to create the Certificate of Trust in Existence and Authority, I used ChatGPT to draft the initial document.

I then hired a Legal Document Preparer (LDP) to review my draft, along with the Will and trust, to ensure it complied with state laws. The LDP made any necessary changes and recorded the document for me, which cost only $25.

The LDP charged $150 to prepare the document, and I paid an additional $10 to have it notarized. This approach saved me both time and money compared to hiring an attorney for the entire process.

Below is a template for creating the certificate. If you are reading the e-book, you can copy and paste this template into ChatGPT and upload the Will and trust document to personalize it. Use the prompt provided below.

Template: Certificate of Trust in Existence and Authority

State of [State]
County of [County Name]

I. Declaration
This Certificate of Trust is executed to confirm the existence of the trust described below and to provide information about the trust and the authority of the trustee(s). This document is provided in accordance with applicable state laws to serve as verification of the trust's existence and the trustee's authority.

II. Trust Information

- Name of Trust: [Name of Trust]

- Date of Trust: [Trust Date]

- Settlor(s): [Settlor Name(s)]

- Current Trustee(s): [Trustee Name(s)]

- Successor Trustee(s): [Names of Successor Trustees, if applicable, as listed in the trust]

III. Trust Status

- The trust is currently in existence and has not been revoked, modified, or amended in any manner that would invalidate this Certificate.

- The trust is [revocable/irrevocable].

IV. Trustee's Authority

The trustee is authorized to act on behalf of the trust in accordance with its terms and applicable state laws.

Specific authority includes but is not limited to the power to:

- Sell, convey, and transfer real estate and other trust assets.

- Manage and administer trust property.

- Execute all necessary documents to carry out the powers described above.

V. Property Held in Trust

The trust holds title to certain assets, including but not limited to the following:

- Real Property: [Address of Property, e.g., 123 Main Street, City, State, ZIP]

- Additional assets as detailed in the trust documents.

VI. Representations

No court proceedings are pending for the administration of this trust.

This Certificate is being executed to confirm the authority of the trustee to act on behalf of the trust and to provide assurance to third parties dealing with the trustee.

Third parties may rely on this Certificate as conclusive proof of the trustee's authority.

VII. Trustee's Signature

I, [Trustee Name], as trustee of [Name of Trust], declare under penalty of perjury under the laws of the State of [State] that the statements made in this Certificate are true and correct to the best of my knowledge.

Dated: [Date]

Signed:
[Trustee Name]
Trustee

VIII. Notary Acknowledgment
State of [State]
County of [County Name]

On this [Date] day of [Month], [Year], before me, a Notary Public, personally appeared [Trustee Name], known to me (or proved to me on the basis of satisfactory evidence) to be the person whose name is subscribed to this instrument and acknowledged to me that they executed the same in their authorized capacity, and that by their signature on the instrument, they executed it on behalf of the trust.

Witness my hand and official seal:

[Notary Signature]
[Notary Printed Name]
Notary Public, State of [State]
My Commission Expires: [Expiration Date]

Notes

1. Replace bracketed placeholders ([ ]) with specific information from your trust.

2. Verify with local laws or institutions to ensure compliance with your state's requirements.

3. Use this document for banks, title companies, or any party requiring proof of the trust's existence and the trustee's authority.

Prompt for ChatGPT

If you are using ChatGPT to create this document, copy and paste the following prompt:

"Using the template below, create a Certificate of Trust in Existence and Authority for me. I will upload my trust and Will documents for reference. Please include all necessary details, including the trust's name, date of execution, settlor(s), trustee(s), and confirmation of trustee authority. Ensure it complies with applicable laws in the state of [Enter state the trust is in] and is ready for notarization."

By creating this certificate, you will have a powerful tool to navigate your responsibilities as trustee efficiently. In the next chapter, we will discuss securing the deceased's assets in detail.

What If You Are the Successor Trustee?

If you are the successor trustee named in the trust and the original trustee has passed away or is unable to serve, an additional document may be required to formally recognize your authority.

This document is commonly referred to as an **Affidavit of Successor Trustee**.

What Is the Affidavit of Successor Trustee?

The Affidavit of Successor Trustee is a legal document that verifies:

- The original trustee is no longer serving (due to death, resignation, or incapacity).

- You, as the successor trustee, are now authorized to act on behalf of the trust.

This document is important because it:

- Provides proof of the original trustee's status (e.g., deceased).

- Officially confirms your appointment as the successor trustee.

- Ensures third parties, such as financial institutions or title companies, recognize your authority to manage or transfer trust assets.

Why Do You Need It?

The affidavit is often required when:

- The trust involves financial accounts or real estate transactions.

- Institutions need additional assurance beyond the Certificate of Trust.

Below is a template you can use to create an Affidavit of Successor Trustee. If you are reading the e-book, you can copy and paste this template into ChatGPT and upload your trust and Will documents to personalize it.

Affidavit of Successor Trustee Template

Affidavit of Successor Trustee

State of [State]
County of [County Name]

I, [Your Full Name], being duly sworn, declare as follows:

1. **Trust Information**:

   o   Name of Trust: [Name of Trust]

   o   Date of Trust: [Trust Date]

   o   Settlor(s): [Settlor Name(s)]

2. **Original Trustee**:

   o   Name of Original Trustee: [Original Trustee Name]

   o   Reason for Succession: [Death/Resignation/Incapacity of Original Trustee]

3. **Successor Trustee**:

   o   Pursuant to the terms of the trust, I, [Your Full Name], am named as the successor trustee and have accepted this appointment.

4. **Authority**:

   o   As the successor trustee, I am authorized to act on behalf of the trust in accordance with its terms and applicable law. My authority includes, but is not limited to:

   ▪   Managing, transferring, and distributing trust assets.

- Executing documents necessary to carry out the trust's administration.

5. **Representations**:

- The trust is currently in existence and has not been revoked, modified, or amended in any manner that would invalidate this affidavit.

- No court proceedings are pending for the administration of this trust.

I declare under penalty of perjury under the laws of the State of [State] that the foregoing is true and correct to the best of my knowledge.

Dated: [Date]

Signed:
[Your Full Name]
Successor Trustee

Notary Acknowledgment

State of [State]
County of [County Name]

On this [Date] day of [Month], [Year], before me, a Notary Public, personally appeared [Your Full Name], known to me (or proved to me on the basis of satisfactory evidence) to be the person whose name is subscribed to this instrument and acknowledged to me that they executed the same in their authorized capacity, and that by their signature on the instrument, they executed it on behalf of the trust.

Witness my hand and official seal:

[Notary Signature]
[Notary Printed Name]
Notary Public, State of [State]
My Commission Expires: [Expiration Date]

Prompt for ChatGPT

If you are using ChatGPT to create this document, copy and paste the following prompt:

"Using the template below, create an Affidavit of Successor Trustee for me. I will upload my trust and Will documents for reference. Please include all necessary details, such as the trust's name, date of execution, settlor(s), original trustee, reason for succession, and confirmation of my authority as the successor trustee. Ensure it complies with general state requirements and is ready for notarization."

Practical Advice

- **Documentation**: To prepare this affidavit, you will need supporting documents, such as the original trustee's death certificate (if applicable) and the trust document.

- **Review by an LDP or Attorney**: You may want to have the affidavit reviewed by a Legal Document Preparer (LDP) or attorney to ensure compliance with state laws.

- **Filing**: Some institutions may require the affidavit to be filed or recorded, especially for real estate transactions. Confirm with the relevant party if filing is necessary.

Letters Testamentary
What They Are and Why Executors Need Them

What Are Letters Testamentary?

Letters Testamentary is a legal document issued by the probate court that grants an **Executor** the official authority to act on behalf of a deceased person's estate. This document confirms the Executor's power to manage estate assets, settle debts, and distribute property according to the terms of the Will.

In essence, it is **proof of the Executor's authority**, similar to how a **Certificate of Trust** functions for Trustees. Financial institutions, government agencies, and other entities often require **Letters Testamentary** before allowing the Executor to handle the deceased's assets.

When Are Letters Testamentary Needed?

Letters Testamentary are required in many estate administrations but **not always necessary**. Whether an Executor needs them depends on the following factors:

Situations Where Letters Testamentary Are Required:

- **The estate includes assets that must go through probate.**

    o If the deceased owned real estate, bank accounts, or other significant assets **solely in their name** (with no named beneficiaries or joint owners), probate is typically required, and the court will issue Letters Testamentary.

- **Financial institutions require proof of authority.**

  - o Banks, investment firms, and insurance companies often **will not release funds** or allow account access without Letters Testamentary.

- **The Executor needs to sell or transfer estate assets.**

  - o If real estate, vehicles, or valuable personal property need to be sold or transferred, the title company or DMV may require Letters Testamentary before processing transactions.

- **The estate is involved in legal matters.**

  - o If there are **creditor claims, lawsuits, or disputes among beneficiaries**, Letters Testamentary confirm the Executor's legal ability to represent the estate.

Situations Where Letters Testamentary Are NOT Required

- **The deceased had a fully funded trust.**

  o If all assets were placed in a living trust, the **Successor Trustee** can manage them without probate, making Letters Testamentary unnecessary.

- **All assets had named beneficiaries or joint owners.**

  o If the deceased's financial accounts, real estate, or retirement funds had a **Transfer-on-Death (TOD), Payable-on-Death (POD), or joint ownership designation**, these assets pass directly to beneficiaries outside probate.

- **The estate qualifies for simplified probate or a small estate affidavit.**

  o Many states allow smaller estates (under a certain dollar amount) to be administered using a **small estate affidavit** instead of full probate. In these cases, Letters Testamentary may not be necessary.

Steps to Obtain Letters Testamentary

If you are named as an **Executor**, follow these steps to obtain **Letters Testamentary**:

Step 1: File a Petition for Probate

To begin the probate process and receive **Letters Testamentary**, the Executor must **file a Petition for Probate** with the probate court in the county where the deceased lived.

Gather the Required Documents

Before filing, collect the following documents:

The Original Will – If a Will exists, you must submit the original document to the court. If the Will cannot be located, consult an attorney to determine next steps.

Certified Death Certificate – Obtain copies from the funeral home or the county's vital records office.

Executor's Identification – Your state-issued ID or driver's license.

List of the Deceased's Assets and Debts – This may include real estate, bank accounts, investments, debts, and outstanding bills.

List of Beneficiaries and Heirs – Full names, addresses, and relationships to the deceased.

Petition for Probate Form – This is the formal request to open probate and appoint the Executor. The form's title varies by state, such as "Petition for Probate" or "Application for Letters Testamentary."

Executor's Oath and Bond (if required) – Some states require the Executor to take an oath of office and possibly obtain a bond (insurance) to protect beneficiaries.

Complete the Probate Forms

Each probate court has specific forms, but common ones include:

- **Petition for Probate or Letters Testamentary** – The formal request for appointment as Executor.

- **Notice of Probate** – A document informing beneficiaries and heirs that probate is being initiated.

- **Inventory of Assets** – A preliminary listing of the deceased's property.

- **Oath of Personal Representative** – A sworn statement agreeing to fulfill Executor duties.

Submit the Forms to the Probate Court

- Locate the correct **probate court** (Google "[County Name] Probate Court" to find the appropriate filing location).

- File the completed forms in person, by mail, or online (if allowed in your state).

- Pay the filing fee, which typically ranges from **$250–$500** but varies by state.

Receive a Hearing Date (If Required)

- Some states require a **probate hearing** where the judge will review the Will, confirm the Executor's appointment, and address any challenges.

- If no one contests the Will, this is usually a simple administrative step.

Step 2: Publish and Serve Notice of Probate

Once the probate court accepts the petition, the Executor must notify interested parties:

- **Beneficiaries and Heirs** – Send a formal notice informing them that probate is underway.

- **Creditors** – Publish a **Notice to Creditors** in a local newspaper to alert potential claimants.

- **Government Agencies (if applicable)** – Notify Medicaid, Social Security, and other agencies, if required.

Some courts require proof that these notices have been sent before issuing **Letters Testamentary**.

Step 3: Obtain the Letters Testamentary

- If no objections are raised, the probate court will issue **Letters Testamentary**, granting you the legal authority to act as Executor.
- Request **certified copies** from the court (some banks and institutions require them).

Step 4: Use the Letters Testamentary to Manage the Estate

Once received, use **Letters Testamentary** to:

- **Access Bank Accounts** – Provide a certified copy to the deceased's bank to transfer funds.

- **Sell or Transfer Property** – Title companies require these letters to transfer real estate.

- **Settle Debts and Taxes** – Present them to creditors, the IRS, and other entities.

- **Distribute Inheritances** – Financial institutions will need this document before releasing funds to beneficiaries.

Step 5: Notarization (If Required by Financial Institutions)

- Some banks or government agencies may require **Letters Testamentary** to be notarized before they accept them.

- Visit a **notary public** to get a notarized copy if necessary.

Letters Testamentary Request Template

Below is a basic template for requesting **Letters Testamentary** from the probate court:

[Probate Court Name]
[Address]
[City, State, ZIP Code]
[Date]

Re: Estate of **[Deceased's Full Name]**
Case Number: **[Leave blank for court assignment]**

PETITION FOR LETTERS TESTAMENTARY

I, **[Your Full Name]**, respectfully request that the court issue **Letters Testamentary** appointing me as the Executor of the estate of **[Deceased's Full Name]**, who passed away on **[Date of Death]**.

Attached to this petition are:

- A certified copy of the deceased's **death certificate**.
- The original **Last Will and Testament** of the deceased.
- An inventory of the deceased's assets and liabilities.
- The necessary filing fee of **[$XXX]**.

I affirm that I am willing and able to fulfill my duties as Executor and will act in accordance with the law and the best interests of the estate's beneficiaries.

Sincerely,

[Your Full Name]
Executor of the Estate of **[Deceased's Full Name]**
[Your Address]
[Your Contact Information]

Practical Advice for Executors

- **Obtain Multiple Copies**: Many institutions require an **original certified copy**, not a photocopy, so request at least **5-10 copies** from the court.

- **Check with financial institutions early.** Some banks may have additional forms or requirements before releasing funds, even with Letters Testamentary.

- **Check State-Specific Requirements**: Some states may require additional forms or supporting documents.

- **Keep Records**: Maintain copies of all documents you submit to the probate court.

- **Use Certified Mail**: If mailing documents to the court, send them via certified mail with return receipt requested.

- **Consult an Attorney if Needed**: If the estate involves significant assets, disputes, or legal complications, consulting an estate attorney can help streamline the process

Final Thoughts

Obtaining **Letters Testamentary** is a **critical first step** in estate administration. Following the correct procedures ensures you can legally manage the deceased's assets, settle debts, and distribute inheritances. If you are unsure about the process, **consult your local probate court or a legal professional** to ensure compliance with state laws.

Chapter 6
Secure the Deceased's Assets

One of the most critical steps in administering an estate or trust is securing the deceased's assets.

As an **Executor** or **Trustee**, your responsibility is to locate, protect, and manage these assets until all debts are settled and distributions can be made. Failing to secure assets promptly can lead to loss, disputes, or financial complications.

This chapter will walk you through the process of identifying, securing, and maintaining all types of assets, including real estate, financial accounts, personal property, and investments. You will also learn how to determine which assets belong to the trust and which may require probate.

Why Securing Assets Is Crucial

- **Preserve Value**: Protect assets from loss, damage, or theft.

- **Ensure Proper Distribution**: Confirm which assets are part of the trust and which are not to prevent legal issues.

- **Pay Debts and Taxes**: Assets in the trust must be used to settle outstanding obligations before distribution to beneficiaries.

How to Secure Assets: A Step-by-Step Guide

Step 1: Take Inventory of All Assets

Before you can manage or distribute the estate's assets, you need a clear picture of everything owned by the deceased. The best way to do this is by creating a **comprehensive inventory**.

What to Include in the Inventory:

- **Real Estate**:

    o Locate property deeds to determine ownership. If the deed includes the trust's name, the property is part of the trust. If not, it may require probate.

    o To confirm ownership, contact the county recorder's office or review the property title.

- **Bank Accounts**:

    o Check account statements and verify whether accounts are titled in the name of the trust.

    o For non-trust accounts, you may need to initiate probate if there is no payable-on-death (POD) beneficiary listed.

- **Retirement Accounts**:

  - o Verify the named beneficiaries on accounts such as IRAs, 401(k)s, or pensions. These typically pass directly to the named beneficiary and are not part of the trust unless explicitly stated.

- **Life Insurance**:

  - o Contact the insurance company to confirm the beneficiaries. Policies with named beneficiaries bypass the trust.

- **Personal Property**:

  - o Include valuables such as vehicles, jewelry, art, furniture, and collectibles. As well as Vehicles, Boats, RVs, Motorcycles along with titles and loan documents. Check the trust document to see if these items are explicitly listed.

- **Other Investments**:

  - **Identify stocks, bonds, or mutual funds.** Check ownership and confirm if they are held in the trust's name.

  - **Business Interests** (LLCs, partnerships, stock in privately held companies)

  - **Outstanding Debts** (mortgages, credit cards, loans, medical bills)

  - **Safe Deposit Boxes** and Cash Holdings

  Digital Assets (cryptocurrency, online financial accounts, digital business assets)

How to Locate Asset Information:

- Review financial statements and tax returns.

- Check mail and emails for account notifications.

- Contact banks, investment firms, and insurance companies.

- Search personal files, safes, and safe deposit boxes.

- Request a **credit report** to uncover unknown debts or accounts.

Step 2: Determine If Assets Are in the Trust or Estate

Some assets may be held in a **trust**, while others are part of the **probate estate**. Understanding the distinction is crucial for handling them correctly.

How to Identify Trust vs. Estate Assets

- **Trust Assets:**

    o Typically, assets with titles in the trust's name (e.g., "John Doe Living Trust")

    o Properties, bank accounts, or investments explicitly transferred into the trust

    o Life insurance policies or retirement accounts listing the trust as a beneficiary

- **Estate (Probate) Assets:**

  - Assets titled solely in the deceased's name without a beneficiary designation

  - Any real estate not deeded to the trust

  - Personal property that does not have a designated ownership title

Why This Matters:

- **Trust Assets**: Can be managed and distributed by the **Trustee** without probate.

- **Probate Assets**: Must go through the probate court process before they can be transferred.

How to Determine If Real Estate Is in the Trust

- **Locate the Property Deed**:

  - o To find the property deed, start by contacting the county recorder's office where the property is located. Most counties allow you to search their public records online using the property address or the owner's name.

  - o Alternatively, you can hire a title company or a Legal Document Preparer (LDP) to assist with locating the deed.

- **Check Ownership**:

  - o Review the deed to see if it lists the trust as the owner. This may be indicated by wording such as "[Name of Trustee], as Trustee of [Name of Trust]."

  - o If the trust's name does not appear on the deed, the property is likely not part of the trust and may require probate.

- **Confirm with the County Recorder's Office**:

  - Visit or call the recorder's office to verify the deed's current ownership status. Many offices can provide certified copies of the deed for a small fee.

  - If you're uncertain about interpreting the deed, consult an attorney or LDP for clarification.

- **What to Do If the Property Is Not in the Trust**:

  - If the trust document references the property but the deed does not list the trust, you may need to use probate or file a **"Heggstad Petition"** in certain states, such as California, to transfer the property into the trust retroactively.

What Is a Heggstad Petition?

A Heggstad Petition is a legal request to the court asking for property to be declared part of a trust, even if the title was never formally transferred to the trust during the settlor's lifetime.

It is based on the premise that the settlor intended the property to be part of the trust but failed to complete the necessary paperwork.

States Where a Heggstad Petition May Apply

This petition is most commonly used in California, but other states may have similar processes or legal mechanisms to achieve the same result. Consult with an attorney to determine whether this applies in your state.

Steps to Obtain a Heggstad Petition

1. **Consult an Attorney or a LDP**:

   - This process is complex and typically requires the assistance of an estate attorney to draft and file the petition.

   - Legal Document Preparer (LDP) can assist in drafting a Heggstad Petition, as they specialize in creating legal documents based on your direction. However, because a Heggstad Petition involves a legal request to the court and requires evidence to establish the settlor's intent, you should consult with an estate attorney to ensure accuracy and compliance with local court requirements. An LDP can prepare the necessary documents for you, which may save costs compared to hiring an attorney for the entire process.

2. **Provide Evidence**:

   - Submit evidence showing the settlor's intent to include the property in the trust, such as:

     - Language in the trust document referencing the property.

     - Correspondence or records indicating the settlor's intent.

3. **File the Petition**:

   - File the with the probate court in the county where the trust or property is located.

4. **Attend the Hearing**:

   - A court hearing may be required to review and approve the petition.

5. **Implement the Court Order**:

   - If approved, the court's order will direct that the property be transferred into the trust, resolving any ownership ambiguity.

On the following page is a general template for a Heggstad Petition. Keep in mind that this template may need to be customized to comply with local court rules and requirements.

Heggstad Petition Template

[Court Name, e.g., Superior Court of California, County of [County Name]]

In the Matter of the [Name of Trust]

Case No. [Case Number, if applicable]

HEGGSTAD PETITION TO CONFIRM TITLE TO PROPERTY IN TRUST

Petitioner:
[Your Full Name], as Successor Trustee of the [Name of Trust, e.g., John Doe Revocable Living Trust dated [Date]].

Petitioner Alleges:

1. **Trust Establishment and Purpose**:
   [Name of Settlor] created the [Name of Trust] on [Date], for the purpose of managing and distributing the trust assets as described in the trust document. A copy of the trust is attached as Exhibit A.

2. **Trustee Appointment**:
   Petitioner, [Your Full Name], is the duly appointed successor trustee under the terms of the trust and has accepted this role. Evidence of the successor trustee's appointment is attached as Exhibit B.

3. **Property Description**:
   The property located at [Address or Description of Real Estate, e.g., 123 Main Street, City, State, ZIP], identified as [Legal Description of Property from Deed], is the subject of this petition. A copy of the deed is attached as Exhibit C.

4. **Intent to Transfer Property**:
   At the time of the trust's creation, [Name of Settlor] intended for the property described above to be part of the trust's assets. The trust document explicitly references the property or expresses the settlor's intent to include all real property in the trust.

5. **Relief Requested**:

Petitioner requests that the court confirm that the property described herein is part of the [Name of Trust] and under the management and authority of the successor trustee.

Prayer for Relief:

WHEREFORE, Petitioner respectfully requests that the court:

1. Confirm that the property located at [Address or Description of Real Estate] is part of the [Name of Trust].
2. Authorize the trustee to manage and administer the property under the terms of the trust.
3. Grant any other relief the court deems appropriate.

Dated: [Date]

Signed:

[Your Full Name]

Successor Trustee of [Name of Trust]

Verification:

I, [Your Full Name], declare under penalty of perjury under the laws of the State of [State] that the foregoing is true and correct to the best of my knowledge.

Signed:

[Your Full Name]

Date: [Date]

[Notary Acknowledgment Section, if required by your court rules]

A Heggstad Petition can save time and money by avoiding full probate proceedings, but it requires clear evidence and legal expertise to succeed.

Step 3: Organize Documentation

For each asset, collect supporting documents:

- Property deeds and titles.

- Bank statements and account details.

- Investment account summaries.

- Retirement account beneficiary designations.

- Life insurance policies.

- Personal property appraisals (if applicable).

Keep these documents organized in a secure location or digital file. Consider using a spreadsheet or worksheet to track the following information:

Asset Type	Description	Value	Trust-Owned?	Notes
Real Estate	123 Main St., Phoenix, AZ	$300,000	Yes	In trust deed confirmed.
Bank Account	Checking Account, XYZ Bank	$50,000	Yes	Titled in trust's name.
Retirement Account	IRA, Fidelity	$200,000	No	Beneficiary: John Doe.

Step 4: Secure Real Estate and Physical Assets

Real Estate

If the deceased owned real estate, securing the property is a priority.

Key Steps:

1. **Change the Locks** – Prevent unauthorized access.

2. **Ensure Home Insurance is Active** – Notify the insurance company of the owner's passing to maintain coverage.

3. **Maintain Utilities** – Keep electricity, water, and heat running to prevent damage.

4. **Inspect the Property** – Look for maintenance issues, leaks, or potential hazards.

5.   **Monitor Mail** – Redirect mail to your address to track financial obligations and account notifications.

Vehicles, Boats, and Other High-Value Property

1. Locate the **titles** and confirm ownership.

2. If needed, **store vehicles in a secure location**.

3. Maintain insurance until the assets are transferred or sold.

Personal Property

- Document valuable items with **photos** or **videos**.

- Secure small, high-value items like **jewelry, cash, and collectibles**.

- Consider hiring an **appraiser** for unique or expensive belongings.

Step 5: Open a Trust or Estate Bank Account

If you are a **Trustee**, you will need to open a bank account in the **trust's name** to manage its assets.

If you are an **Executor**, you may need to open an **estate bank account** to handle assets that are subject to probate.

116

For Trustees: Opening a Trust Bank Account

- If not already done, open a **bank account in the trust's name** to manage all financial transactions.

- This account will be used to **deposit proceeds from real estate sales, collect income, and pay expenses** related to the trust.

- You will typically need:

  o A **Certificate of Trust in Existence and Authority** (or the full trust document, depending on the bank's requirements).

  o A certified **death certificate** of the settlor.

  o A **Tax ID Number (EIN)** for the trust (unless the trust is revocable and still using the settlor's SSN).

For Executors: Opening an Estate Bank Account (if needed)

- If you are also the **Executor**, and assets must go through probate, you may need to open a **separate estate bank account** in the name of the decedent's estate.

- This account is used to **receive probate assets, pay estate debts, and distribute funds to heirs**.

- You will typically need:
    - **Letters Testamentary** from the probate court granting you authority to act on behalf of the estate.

    - A certified **death certificate** of the decedent.

    - A **Tax ID Number (EIN)** for the estate (required for estates in probate).

What If You Are Both the Trustee and Executor?

- If all assets are **held in the trust**, you **do not** need to open an estate bank account—just use the trust account.

- If **some assets are in the trust and others are in probate**, you may need **both** a trust account and an estate account to properly manage the separate funds.

- Keep **trust funds and estate funds separate** to avoid legal and tax complications.

Practical Advice

- Check with the financial institution about their specific requirements for opening either type of account.

- Maintain detailed records of all deposits and withdrawals to avoid legal issues or beneficiary disputes.

- Consult an attorney or CPA if you're unsure whether an estate account is required in your situation.

Step 6: Manage Financial Accounts

Bank and Investment Accounts

- **For Trust Accounts:**

  o Provide the **Certificate of Trust** and death certificate to banks to gain access.

- **For Probate Accounts:**

  o Provide **Letters Testamentary** to gain control over the estate's financial assets.

- **Joint Accounts with Right of Survivorship** automatically pass to the co-owner.

- **Payable-on-Death (POD) Accounts** go directly to the named beneficiary.

Retirement Accounts & Life Insurance

- **Verify beneficiary designations.**

- Contact the financial institution to **initiate claim forms**.

- Do **not** move funds into the estate unless legally required.

Safe Deposit Boxes

- If the deceased had a **safe deposit box**, you may need:

    o A court order (if probate assets are inside)

    o Proof of authority as executor or trustee

Step 7: Monitor Cash Flow: Managing Trust and Estate Expenses

Managing cash flow is essential to ensure all obligations—such as debts, taxes, and administrative costs—are paid correctly. The account you use will depend on whether you are handling a **trust, an estate, or both.**

For Trustees: Using the Trust Bank Account

- Use the **trust's bank account** to **pay ongoing expenses related to trust assets**, including:
    - Property taxes, insurance, and maintenance for real estate held in the trust.

    - Trust administration costs, such as accountant or legal fees.

    - Taxes owed by the trust (if applicable).

    - Distributions to beneficiaries as outlined in the trust.

Do **not** mix personal funds with trust funds—always keep transactions separate.

For Executors: Using the Estate Bank Account (if probate is involved)

- If you are administering a **probate estate**, use the **estate bank account** to **pay estate-related expenses**, including:
    - Funeral and burial costs (if not prepaid or covered by life insurance).

    - Court filing fees and probate attorney fees (if applicable).

    - Debts owed by the decedent (medical bills, credit card debts, etc.).

    - Estate taxes or final income taxes for the decedent.

The **estate account should only be used for probate assets**—do not pay trust expenses from the estate account.

What If You Are Both the Trustee and the Executor?

- If **all assets are in the trust**, then only the **trust account** is needed to manage expenses.

- If **some assets are in probate**, you may need **both** a trust account and an estate account.

- **Never combine funds** from both accounts—each must be used for its own specific purpose.

Practical Advice

- **Track every expense** to provide an accurate accounting to beneficiaries and the court (if probate is required).

- **Set up online banking access** for easy monitoring of transactions and payments.

- **Work with a CPA** to ensure that taxes and distributions are handled correctly.

- If you're unsure which account should cover an expense, **consult an attorney or tax professional** before making payments.

Step 8: Pay Debts and Taxes

Before distributing assets, debts must be **settled in a legally required order**:

1. **Funeral and Burial Costs**

2. **Outstanding Taxes** (Federal and State Income Tax, Property Tax, Estate Tax)

3. **Secured Debts** (Mortgages, Car Loans, Home Equity Loans)

4. **Unsecured Debts** (Credit Cards, Medical Bills, Personal Loans)

Negotiating or Settling Debts

To negotiate debt for a deceased person, follow these steps:

1. **Confirm the debt's authenticity:**
   - Review financial records to ensure the debt wasn't already paid.

   - Request a statement or letter from creditors showing the outstanding balance.

2. **Notify creditors of the death:**
   - Inform them that you're handling the estate.

   - Provide executor or administrator contact details.

3. **Understand your rights and responsibilities:**
    - Know that family members aren't typically respon-sible for the deceased's debts unless they co-signed or are in community property states.

    - Be aware that debt collectors can only discuss debts with specific individuals like spouses, executors, or administrators.

4. **Prepare a settlement offer:**
    - Determine the maximum amount the estate can af-ford to pay.

5. **Negotiate with creditors:**
    - Contact creditors and present your settlement offer.

    - Be prepared to discuss and reach an agreement.

6. **For medical bills:**
    - Request itemized bills to verify charges.

    - Check insurance coverage thoroughly.

    - Negotiate with healthcare providers for reduced bills or payment plans.

7. **Get agreements in writing**
   - Ensure all negotiated settlements are documented.

8. **Make payments from the estate**
   - Use estate assets to pay agreed-upon amounts.

   - Keep records of all payments and agreements.

Step 9: When Can Assets Be Distributed?

Trust Assets:

- Can be distributed once debts and expenses have been settled.

- Must follow the trust's instructions on timing and allocation.

Probate Assets:

- Cannot be distributed until probate is complete and the court authorizes asset transfers.

- Executors must file a **Final Accounting** before closing the estate.

Final Checklist: Securing the Deceased's Assets

1. Create an Inventory

☑ List all assets (real estate, accounts, Retirement accounts, Life insurance policies, personal property, debts).

☑ Locate ownership documents and titles.

☑ Photograph valuable property for records.

2. Organize Documentation:

☑ Deeds and titles

☑ Financial statements

☑ Beneficiary designations

☑ Insurance policies

2. Secure Physical Assets

☑ Lock and insure real estate.

☑ Store valuables safely.

☑ Protect vehicles and ensure they are properly titled.

3. Manage Financial Accounts

☑ Contact banks and investment firms.

☑ Provide necessary legal documents (Will, Trust, Letters Testamentary).

☑ Verify and claim life insurance or retirement accounts.

4. Settle Debts and Liabilities

☑ Identify and notify creditors.

☑ Negotiate where possible.

☑ Pay outstanding balances in the correct legal order.

5. Prepare for Distribution

☑ Ensure all debts and expenses are cleared.

☑ Follow the trust's or estate's instructions for distributions.

☑ Retain records for legal and tax purposes.

By following these steps, you will ensure the deceased's assets are properly secured, debts are handled, and beneficiaries receive their rightful inheritances in a legally sound manner.

Chapter 7
Notifying Beneficiaries

One of the most crucial responsibilities as an Executor or Trustee is ensuring that all beneficiaries are properly notified about their interests in the estate or trust.

This step ensures that everyone named in the trust is informed of their role and rights. Proper notification sets the stage for trust administration and minimizes the risk of disputes later on.

This chapter will guide you through the process of notifying beneficiaries, including:

- Writing and sending notification letters.

- Handling disputes or questions from beneficiaries.

- Documenting your communications.

Why Notification Is Important

- **Legal Compliance**: Most states require executors and trustees to notify beneficiaries within a specific timeframe after the settlor's death. Failing to do so can lead to legal complications.

- **Transparency**: Providing timely and clear communication reassures beneficiaries that the estate or trust is being managed appropriately and ethically.

- **Prevents Disputes**: Beneficiaries who feel informed are less likely to challenge the estate or trust administration process.

How to Notify Beneficiaries: Step-by-Step

1. **Review the Estate or Trust Documents:**

   o Identify all beneficiaries named, including contingent beneficiaries.

   o Note specific instructions regarding beneficiary rights, distributions, or conditions set by the deceased.

2. **Draft Notification Letters**:

   o Write formal letters to each beneficiary, explaining their role and rights under the trust.

   o Include relevant details, such as:

     ▪ The name and date of the trust or will.

- The trustee's name and contact information.

- A summary of their inheritance or role (if applicable).

- A copy of the trust or will document (if required by state law).

3. **Send Letters**:

   o Send the notification letters via **certified mail with return receipt requested** to ensure delivery.

   o Keep copies of the letters and delivery confirmations for your records.

4. **Allow Time for Questions**:

   o After sending the notifications, give beneficiaries time to ask questions or request additional information.

   o Respond promptly and professionally to all inquiries.

5. **Document Everything**:

   ○ Maintain a record of all communications, including letters, emails, and phone calls.

   ○ Use a **Communication Log Worksheet** (template provided below).

Beneficiary Notification Letter Template

[Your Full Name]
Executor/Trustee of **[Name of Trust/Estate]**
[Your Address]
[City, State, ZIP Code]
[Date]

[Beneficiary's Full Name]
[Beneficiary's Address]
[City, State, ZIP Code]

Subject: Notification of Beneficiary Status under [Name of Trust/Estate]

Dear [Beneficiary's Name],

I am writing to formally notify you that **[Settlor/Decedent's Full Name]**, the [settlor/testator] of **[Name of Trust or Estate]**, passed away on **[Date of Death]**. As the appointed [Trustee/Executor], it is my responsibility to inform you of your rights and interests under the **[Trust or Will]**.

Trust/Estate Details:

- Name of Trust/Estate: **[Name of Trust/Estate]**

- Date of Execution: **[Date of Trust or Will]**

- Your Status: **[Describe the beneficiary's role (e.g., primary beneficiary, contingent beneficiary)]**

Under the terms of the **[Trust or Will]**, you are entitled to **[describe the specific inheritance or role in the trust/estate]**. Enclosed is **[a copy of the trust/will OR the relevant sections pertaining to your inheritance]** for your review.

If you have any questions regarding this matter, please do not hesitate to contact me at **[Your Phone Number]** or **[Your Email Address]**.

Sincerely,
[Your Full Name]
Executor/Trustee of **[Name of Trust/Estate]**

Handling Disputes or Questions from Beneficiaries

It is common for beneficiaries to have questions or concerns. Some may even challenge aspects of the estate or trust. Here's how to manage these situations professionally:

1. **Stay Calm and Professional**:

    ○   Maintain a neutral and respectful tone in all interactions.

    ○   Provide factual responses based on the estate or trust document.

2. **Refer to the Legal Documents:**

    ○   If a dispute arises, direct the beneficiary to the relevant section of the will or trust that explains their inheritance.

    ○   Avoid interpreting legal clauses—if necessary, refer them to an estate attorney.

3. **Keep Records of Communications**

    ○   Document all interactions in a **Communication Log Worksheet**.

○   If a beneficiary continues to dispute, consider involving a mediator or legal counsel.

4.   **Hold a Beneficiary Meeting (If Needed):**

○   In cases where multiple beneficiaries have concerns, hosting a formal meeting (virtual or in-person) can clarify misunderstandings and prevent conflicts.

5.   **Seek Legal Advice When Necessary:**

○   If a dispute escalates, consult an estate attorney to ensure you are handling the situation correctly and within the law.

6.   **Document the Resolution**:

○   Record the outcome of any dispute resolution efforts, including agreements or actions taken.

Documenting Your Communications

Keeping records of beneficiary communications is essential to protect yourself from future legal issues and disputes.

Communication Log Worksheet

Date	Beneficiary Name	Method of Communication	Summary of Discussion	Actions Taken
MM/ DD/ YYYY	[Beneficiary Name]	Phone/Email/ Letter	[Brief Summary]	[Any Follow-Up Required]

Maintaining a detailed log ensures that you have a clear record of all notifications, questions, and resolutions.

Do Beneficiaries Have the Right to See the Trust or Will?

When notifying beneficiaries, it is important to understand your obligations regarding the disclosure of the trust or Will. Here are some key considerations:

1. **Legal Requirements**:

    o   Some states require trustees to provide beneficiaries with a copy of the trust or at least the relevant portions that pertain to their inheritance.

    o   Ask your estate attorney in the consultation to determine the specific requirements in your state.

2.   What If Beneficiaries Request a Copy?

o   If a beneficiary requests a copy of the trust or Will, assess whether they are legally entitled to view it. Typically, primary beneficiaries (those directly receiving assets) have the right to review the document.

o   If not required, you may provide a **summary** or relevant excerpts. Providing a redacted version or only the relevant sections may be an option, especially if the document contains sensitive information unrelated to their inheritance.

3.   Should You Proactively Share the Full Trust/Will?

o   While transparency is important, sharing the entire trust or Will may not always be necessary or advisable, particularly if it could lead to disputes or reveal confidential information.

o   If you are uncertain, consult with an attorney before disclosing the document.

4. **Best Practices**:

- o **Be Transparent Where Required**: Clearly communicate the portions of the trust relevant to each
  beneficiary.

- o **Document Your Actions**: Keep records of what
  was shared and when to protect yourself from potential liability.

- o **Seek Professional Guidance**: If there is disagree-
  ment or uncertainty about disclosure, involve a legal
  professional to navigate the situation appropriately.

What If You Are the Sole Beneficiary and Trustee?

In some cases, you may find that you are both the trustee and the
sole beneficiary of the trust. This situation typically arises when
there are no other beneficiaries listed in the trust or when other
beneficiaries are deceased.

If you are both the trustee and sole beneficiary, the process is sim-
pler:

- **You still need to document the process properly.**

- **Follow all legal requirements,** such as filing notices and final tax returns.

- **Formally transfer assets to yourself** using proper legal channels (e.g., deed transfers for real estate).

- **File a final accounting document** to close the trust or estate officially.

Here's how to navigate this scenario:

1. **Understand Your Dual Role**:

   ○ As the trustee, you are responsible for administering the trust, paying debts, and settling taxes.

   ○ As the sole beneficiary, you are entitled to receive the remaining assets of the trust once all obligations have been fulfilled.

2. **Determine If Any Additional Steps Are Required**:

   ○ You may still need to notify yourself as the sole beneficiary and document the process for compliance and record-keeping.

- Confirm with an attorney or Legal Document Preparer (LDP) if any additional filings or legal steps are required in your state.

3. **Complete Administrative Duties**:

- Follow the same procedures for paying debts, taxes, and finalizing the trust as outlined in earlier chapters.

- Keep detailed records of all actions taken.

4. **Distribute Assets**:

Once all obligations have been met, you can formally distribute the remaining assets to yourself as the sole beneficiary. To do this:

- **Financial Accounts**: If the trust holds cash or liquid assets, you can transfer the funds to your personal account. Ensure the transfer is properly documented, such as by retaining transaction records or creating a written receipt.

- **Real Estate**: To transfer real estate, you may need to execute a deed transferring the property from the trust to your name. This often requires notarization and recording the deed with the county recorder's office.

o **Personal Property**: For physical assets like vehicles or valuables, maintain a written record of the transfer, including descriptions of the items and their estimated value.

o **Documentation**: Create a distribution statement listing each asset and its value, with a note indicating that you, as the sole beneficiary, received it. This ensures transparency and protects you from future disputes.

o Ask the estate attorney in your consult   if you are unsure of the specific process for any type of asset.

5.   **Close the Trust**:

o Prepare a final accounting and ensure all documentation is in order before closing the trust.

Additional Tips for Success

- **Be Transparent**: Share relevant information openly to build trust.

- **Keep Records**: Detailed documentation protects you from potential liability.

- **Use Professional Help When Needed**: If disputes escalate, don't hesitate to involve legal or mediation professionals.

By following these steps, you can ensure that all beneficiaries are properly notified and that the estate or trust administration process remains transparent and legally compliant.

Next, we will discuss another critical aspect of estate administration—**Notifying Creditors.**

Chapter 8:
Notifying Creditors

One of the most critical steps in estate and trust administration is notifying creditors. Whether you are serving as an **Executor** managing a probate estate or a **Trustee** administering a trust, you must ensure that any outstanding debts are identified and addressed appropriately.

Notifying creditors starts a legal timeframe within which they must submit claims, ultimately protecting the estate or trust from future liability.

This chapter will walk you through the process of identifying creditors, publishing legal notices, handling creditor claims, and ensuring debts are settled in compliance with the law.

Why Notifying Creditors Is Important

1. **Legal Obligation**: Many states require Executors and Trustees to formally notify creditors, providing them an opportunity to file claims.

2. **Protection Against Future Claims:** Once the legal timeframe for claims has expired, any creditor that did not submit a claim forfeits their right to collect, limiting future liability.

3. **Ensures Proper Debt Settlement:** The estate or trust cannot be fully distributed until all valid debts and obligations are resolved.

4. **Prevents Personal Liability:** Executors and Trustees must ensure that all legitimate debts are paid before distributing assets, or they may be held personally liable for unpaid claims.

Known Creditors vs. Unknown Creditors

- **Known Creditors**: Individuals or entities with identifiable claims against the deceased or the trust. These creditors must be notified directly.

- **Unknown Creditors**: Creditors who are not immediately identifiable. Publishing a notice in a newspaper addresses this group by providing public notice of the trust's administration.

Steps for Notifying Creditors

1. Identify Known Creditors:

Start by reviewing the decedent's financial records to determine outstanding debts. Common sources include:

- **Bank Statements** – Identify recurring charges or loan payments.

- **Credit Card Statements** – Determine balances owed.

- **Medical Bills** – Look for outstanding healthcare expenses.

- **Utility Bills** – Verify if any accounts remain open.

- **Loan Agreements** – Check mortgage documents or personal loan records.

- **Tax Records** – Identify past-due state or federal taxes.

Create a **creditor list** with the following details:

- Creditor name and contact information.

- Account number (if available).

- Amount owed.

- Due date and status (paid, disputed, outstanding).

2. Publish a Notice to Creditors:

If the estate is undergoing probate, many states require a **Notice to Creditors** to be published in a newspaper of general circulation within the county where the deceased lived.

Key Information to Include:

- Full name of the deceased.

- Date of death.

- Executor or Trustee's name and contact information.

- Deadline for submitting claims (varies by state, typically **90-120 days**).

- Instructions for submitting claims (mailing address or court information).

Example of a Notice to Creditors

NOTICE TO CREDITORS

In the Matter of the Estate of [Full Name of Decedent], Deceased.

Date of Death: [Date of Death]

Notice is hereby given that [Executor/Trustee Name] is managing the [Estate of / Trust of] [Decedent's Name]. All persons having claims against the estate or trust are required to present their claims in writing to the address provided below within [State-Specific Claim Period] from the date of this notice or be forever barred.

Dated: [Date]

[Executor/Trustee Name]
[Executor/Trustee Address]
[City, State, ZIP Code]
[Phone Number]

Publication Requirements

- Must be published in an approved legal newspaper.

- Typically runs once per week for **three to four consecutive weeks**.

- Obtain and keep a copy of the published notice for records.

When Posting a Public Notice Might Not Be Necessary

Some states waive the requirement to publish a public notice if:

- The estate's value is below a certain threshold.

- The deceased had no debts.

- All creditors are known and have been notified directly.

Consult with an estate attorney to confirm whether a public notice is required in your state.

Timeframe Compliance for Unknown Creditors

When notifying unknown creditors through a public notice, it is essential to comply with the statutory timeframe set by your state. Typically, this timeframe is as follows:

1. **Publication Period**:

   o Most states require the notice to be published for 3-4 consecutive weeks in a newspaper of general circulation.

2. **Claim Filing Deadline**:

   o Creditors usually have a limited window to file claims, often ranging from 4 to 6 months from the date of the first published notice. This timeframe varies by state.

3. **Statutory Bar Date**:

   o Once the deadline has passed, any claims from unknown creditors are barred, meaning they cannot be enforced against the trust or estate.

To ensure compliance:

- Consult your state's laws regarding creditor notification and claim periods.

- Keep a record of the publication dates and retain proof of publication, such as an affidavit from the newspaper.

- Mark the claim deadline clearly in your records to avoid disputes. Even if all creditors are known, publishing a notice to creditors can provide an extra layer of legal protection by addressing unknown claims. This ensures that any undisclosed debts are extinguished after the claim period expires.

Publication Criteria

Key Steps for Publishing a Notice:

1. **Choose a Newspaper**:

   o   Select a newspaper of general circulation in the deceased's county of residence.

   o   Confirm the newspaper meets state requirements for legal notices.

2. **Draft the Notice**:

   o   Use clear and concise language to include all required details.

3. **Submit the Notice**:

   o   Contact the newspaper's legal notice department.

   o   Provide the draft notice, proof of death, and payment for publication fees.

Key Legal Requirements for General Circulation

• The newspaper must be widely distributed within the county.

• It must meet state requirements for publishing legal notices.

• Notices must run for the duration specified by the state law, typically 3-4 weeks.

3. Send Direct Notices to Known Creditors:

All known creditors must be **notified directly** in writing, whether the estate is in probate or not.

How to Notify Creditors:

1. Send a **formal letter** via **certified mail** with a return receipt.

2. Include a copy of the death certificate (if required by the creditor).

3. Provide a deadline for submitting claims (typically **90 days from receipt**).

4. Keep copies of all correspondence and delivery confirmations.

Example of a Direct Notice to Creditors

[Your Full Name]
Executor/Trustee of [Name of Estate/Trust]
[Your Address]
[City, State, ZIP Code]
[Date]

[Creditor's Name]
[Creditor's Address]
[City, State, ZIP Code]

Subject: Official Notice Regarding the Estate/Trust of [Decedent's Name]

Dear [Creditor's Name],

I am writing to inform you that [Decedent's Name] passed away on [Date of Death]. As the [Executor/Trustee] of the [Estate/Trust], I am responsible for identifying and resolving any outstanding debts.

If you have a claim against the [estate/trust], please submit the details in writing, along with any supporting documentation, to the address below no later than [Claim Deadline Date]. Claims submitted after this date may be barred.

If you have any questions, you may contact me at [Your Phone Number] or [Your Email Address].

Sincerely,
[Your Full Name]
Executor/Trustee of [Estate/Trust Name]

4. Handling Creditor Claims:

Once creditors submit claims, they must be reviewed for validity.

Valid Claims:

- o Verify the debt amount against the deceased's records.

- o Ensure that payments are made from the estate/trust bank account.

- o Obtain a written release from the creditor upon payment.

Disputed Claims:

- o Request supporting documentation from the creditor.

- o Consult with an attorney if the claim seems questionable.

- o If necessary, file an objection with the probate court to dispute the claim formally.

Late or Invalid Claims:

- o If a creditor misses the deadline, they **forfeit** the right to collect (subject to state laws).

- o Notify the creditor in writing that the claim has been denied due to untimeliness.

5. Paying Valid Debts:

Once claims are approved, they must be **paid in priority order** using estate or trust funds.

Typical Payment Priority:

1. Funeral and burial expenses.

2. Taxes (income, estate, property taxes).

3. Secured debts (mortgages, car loans).

4. Unsecured debts (credit cards, medical bills).

5. Final distributions to beneficiaries.

What If There Are More Debts Than Assets?

- The estate/trust is considered **insolvent** if debts exceed available funds.

- Do **not** pay any creditors until legal guidance is obtained.

- In probate cases, courts typically establish an order of priority for debt payments.

Practical Advice

- **Document Everything**: Keep meticulous records of all notices sent, claims received, and payments made.

- **Seek Professional Help**: Consult an attorney or Legal Document Preparer (LDP) to ensure compliance with state laws.

- **Use Certified Mail**: Always send direct notices via certified mail to provide proof of delivery.

Key Takeaways

- **Executors and Trustees** must notify creditors and allow them time to file claims.

- **Publishing a Notice to Creditors** is required for probate estates in most states.

- **Direct notices must be sent** to all known creditors by certified mail.

- **Claims must be reviewed** carefully to ensure they are valid before payment.

- **Pay debts in the correct legal order** to avoid personal liability.

- **If the estate is insolvent, consult an attorney before paying any debts.**

By following these steps, you will ensure that all creditor obligations are handled correctly, allowing you to move forward with the estate or trust administration process efficiently and legally.

Chapter 9
Obtain a Tax ID for the Trust

When a trust becomes irrevocable—usually upon the death of the settlor—it is treated as a separate legal entity for tax purposes.

This means it requires an **Employer Identification Number (EIN)** from the IRS to conduct financial transactions, such as managing trust accounts, filing tax returns, or distributing assets.

This chapter explains why an EIN is essential, how to apply for one, and how to use it to manage the trust's financial responsibilities.

Understanding Revocable vs. Irrevocable Trusts

Understanding whether the trust is **revocable** or **irrevocable** is essential to determine if you need an EIN.

1. **Revocable Trust**:

   o   A revocable trust, also known as a living trust, can be altered, amended, or revoked by the settlor (the person who created the trust) at any time during their lifetime.

- While the trust is revocable, it uses the settlor's Social Security number for tax purposes and does not require a separate EIN.

- While the grantor is alive, a revocable trust uses their Social Security Number and does not require an EIN. However, upon the grantor's death, the trust typically becomes irrevocable and needs an EIN.

2. **Irrevocable Trust**:

- An irrevocable trust cannot be changed or revoked once it is established, except under specific circumstances and with court approval.

- It is treated as a separate legal entity for tax purposes and requires an EIN to report income and manage financial transactions.

Knowing whether the trust is revocable or irrevocable will guide your next steps, including applying for an EIN.

What Is an EIN and Why Is It Important?

An EIN functions like a Social Security Number for a business or entity and is required for any trust that must file taxes separately from an individual.

Definition of an EIN:

o   An Employer Identification Number (EIN) is a unique nine-digit number assigned by the IRS to identify a business entity or trust for tax purposes. It functions like a Social Security number but is used for entities rather than individuals.

Why You Need an EIN:

o   **Tax Reporting**: An irrevocable trust must file its own tax returns and report any income it earns. The EIN is used for this purpose.

o   **Financial Transactions**: Banks and financial institutions require an EIN to open a trust bank account.

o   **Legal Compliance**: Obtaining an EIN ensures compliance with federal tax regulations and protects the trustee from personal liability.

How to Apply for an EIN

The easiest way to obtain an EIN is through the **IRS website**, though applications can also be submitted by mail or fax.

1. Prepare Required Information

Gather the following details before applying for an EIN:

- **Trust Name**: The official name of the trust as stated in the trust document.

- **Date Trust Became Irrevocable**: Typically the date of the settlor's death.

- **Trustee Information**: Your name, Social Security number, and contact details.

- **Trust Address**: The mailing address for the trust.

- **Trust Purpose**: For most trusts, this will be "estate or trust administration."

2. Apply Online or By Mail

Online Application (Recommended):

- o Visit the IRS website at https://www.irs.gov.

- o Complete the application form (Form SS-4) through the IRS's online EIN Assistant.

- o Ensure you select "Trust" as the entity type.

- o Submit the application, and you will receive your EIN immediately.

Mail Application:

- o Complete Form SS-4, which can be downloaded from the IRS website.

- o Mail the completed form to the IRS address provided for your state.

- o Processing by mail typically takes 4-6 weeks.

By Fax:

- Complete **Form SS-4** and fax it to the IRS at **(855) 641-6935**.

- Processing time: **4-5 business days**.

Retain Your EIN Confirmation

Save a copy of the confirmation notice for your records. You will need it for financial transactions, tax filings, and opening a trust bank account.

What to Do Once You Have the EIN

Once you have the EIN, you must use it to manage the trust's financial affairs properly.

1. Open a Trust Bank Account: Use the EIN to open a new bank account in the trust's name. This account will be used to manage all trust-related income, expenses, and distributions.

Provide the bank with:

- The trust document.

- The EIN confirmation letter.

- Your identification as the trustee.

2. Notify Financial Institutions

- Contact banks, investment firms, and other entities holding trust assets.

- Update their records with the new EIN and trustee information.

3. File Trust Tax Returns

- Irrevocable trusts must file Form 1041 (U.S. Income Tax Return for Estates and Trusts) annually.

- Consult a tax professional to ensure compliance with tax obligations.

4. Maintain Proper Records

- Keep copies of EIN confirmation letters, tax filings, and trust-related transactions.

- Ensure that all financial activity aligns with the trust's terms and IRS regulations.

Practical Advice

1. **Timing**: Apply for the EIN as soon as the trust becomes irrevocable to avoid delays in managing financial accounts or filing taxes.

2. **Free Process**: Obtaining an EIN directly from the IRS is free. Be cautious of third-party services that charge fees for this process.

3. **Professional Assistance**: If you are unsure about the application process, consult with a Legal Document Preparer (LDP) or tax professional for guidance.

Key Takeaways

- An EIN is required for **irrevocable** trusts but not for revocable trusts before the grantor's death.

- Applying online at **IRS.gov** is the fastest and easiest method.

- The EIN is necessary to open a trust bank account, file tax returns, and manage trust finances.

- Keeping accurate records and consulting a tax professional will help ensure compliance.

By obtaining an EIN promptly and using it to set up the trust's financial accounts, you will ensure the trust's smooth administration and compliance with legal requirements.

Chapter 10
Understanding Probate

Probate is a legal process that governs the administration of a deceased person's estate. It ensures that assets are distributed properly, debts are paid, and legal claims are settled. While probate may seem daunting, understanding its steps can help you manage the process effectively.

In this chapter, we will explore what probate is, when it is required.

We'll also discuss how to navigate the process, including filing the required documents that will minimizing costs and avoid unnecessary expenses by handling much of it without a lawyer, and using strategies to streamline estate settlement.

What Is Probate?

Probate is the **court-supervised** process of settling an estate. The probate court verifies the validity of a Will (if one exists), appoints an **Executor** (if named in the Will) or an **Administrator** (if no Will exists), oversees the payment of debts and taxes, and ensures assets are distributed to the rightful beneficiaries.

When Is Probate Required?

Probate is typically required when:

- The deceased owned assets solely in their name (e.g., bank accounts, real estate).

- There is no valid beneficiary designation for certain accounts or policies.

- The estate includes real estate or large financial holdings without named beneficiaries.

- There are disputes over the Will or estate assets.

- The total value of assets exceeds the state's **small estate threshold** (varies by state).

Examples of Small Estate Thresholds:

- **Arizona**: Estates valued under $75,000 in personal property or $100,000 in real estate may qualify for small estate procedures.

- **California**: The small estate threshold is $184,500 as of 2023.

    o   **Texas**: Estates valued under $75,000 may qualify for a simplified probate process.

Always verify the specific threshold in your state as these amounts may change over time.

When Probate May Not Be Necessary

- Assets are held in a living trust (managed by a **Trustee**).

- Assets are owned jointly with rights of survivorship.

- Accounts have payable-on-death (POD) or transfer-on-death (TOD) designations.

If the deceased had a **living trust**, the **Trustee** handles asset distribution **outside of probate**. However, if any assets were left out of the trust, the **Executor** or **Administrator** may still need to initiate probate to transfer those assets into the trust.

Steps to Start the Probate Process

Step 1: Determine the Need for Probate

- Review all financial documents and asset ownership records.

- Identify assets requiring probate (e.g., real estate, sole-owned bank accounts). Assets titled solely in the decedent's name or lacking beneficiary designations typically need to go through probate.

- Determine if the estate qualifies for **small estate administration** in your state.

- **Trustee's Role:** If the deceased had a trust but left some assets outside of it, the Trustee may need to coordinate with the Executor to transfer those assets.

Step 2: Gather Required Documents

- Collect the following documents:

    o Original Will (if applicable).

    o Certified death certificate.

    o List of the deceased's assets and debts.

o Proof of your relationship to the decedent (if required).

o Contact Information for Heirs & Beneficiaries

Step 3: Determine the Type of Probate

- **Informal Probate**: Suitable for estates with no disputes and a valid Will.

- **Formal Probate**: Required for contested Wills or complex estates.

- **Small Estate Procedures**: If the estate's value is below the state's threshold, you may qualify for a simplified process.

Step 4: File the Probate Application

- Prepare the necessary forms specific to your jurisdiction. (see template below, this can be prepared for a fraction of the cost by a LDP).

- Attach supporting documents:

o Original Will.

o Certified death certificate.

o   Other required proof (e.g., relationship documentation).

- Submit your application to the Probate Clerk's Office.

- Pay the filing fee (approximately \$300-\$350; verify with your local court).

Obtain Court Approval

- The Probate Registrar will review your application and issue Letters of Appointment if approved.

- Address any requests for additional documentation promptly.

Filing Location

To determine where to file your probate application:

- Google: "[County Name] probate court" to locate the Probate Clerk's Office.

- Visit the official website of the court for filing instructions, forms, and fee schedules. Some states offer online probate filing options to simplify the process.

- If filing by mail, confirm the correct mailing address with the court.

Probate Application Template

[Court Name, e.g., Probate Court of [County Name]]

In the Matter of the Estate of:
[Full Name of Decedent]

Case No.: [Leave Blank for Court Use]

Application for Informal Probate

I, [Your Full Name], respectfully request the court to open probate for the estate of [Decedent's Full Name], who passed away on [Date of Death]. As the [Relationship to Decedent, e.g., spouse, child, named executor], I am seeking appointment as the personal representative for this estate.

Attached Documents:

- Original Will (if applicable).

- Certified Death Certificate.

- Supporting documentation.

Signed:
[Your Full Name]
Date: [Date]

Step 5: Appoint a Personal Representative

- If the deceased named an **Executor** in their Will, the court will formally appoint them.

- If no Will exists, the court will appoint an **Administrator** (typically a close relative).

- The representative will receive **Letters Testamentary** or **Letters of Administration**, granting them legal authority to act on behalf of the estate.

- **Trustee's Role:** If assets must be transferred from probate into a trust, the Trustee may need to work with the court-appointed Executor/Administrator.

Step 6: Notify Interested Parties

- **Beneficiaries and Heirs**: Send written notice to all beneficiaries and heirs listed in the Will or required by state law. (As outlines in the previous chapter.)

- **Creditors**: Notify known creditors directly and publish a notice to unknown creditors in a local newspaper.(As outlines in the previous chapter.)

Step 7: Publish Notice to Creditors

- Publish a notice in a newspaper of general circulation in the decedent's county once a week for three consecutive weeks. (As outlines in the previous chapter.)

- Creditors have typically have **3-6 months** (depending on state laws)from the first publication date to submit claims.

- Review and validate creditor claims before making payments.

Step 8: Inventory and Appraise Estate Assets

- File an inventory with the court listing all estate assets and their estimated value. This may require professional appraisals for certain items (e.g., real estate, valuables, and significant assets).

Step 9: Pay Debts & Taxes

- Review creditor claims and settle valid debts using estate funds.

- File and pay final **income tax return** for the deceased and administrative expenses.

- If applicable, file the **estate tax return**.

Step 10: Distribute Assets to Beneficiaries

- Once debts and taxes are cleared, distribute remaining assets per the Will or state intestacy laws if no Will exists.

- **Trustee's Role:** If probate assets must be transferred into a trust first, the Trustee will oversee the final distribution according to the trust's instructions.

Step 11: File a Final Accounting

- Submit a final report to the court detailing all transactions, payments, and distributions made during probate. Request court approval to close the estate.

Step 12: Close the Probate Case

- File a Petition for Discharge to officially close the estate once all obligations are fulfilled.

To officially close an estate after fulfilling all obligations, a **Petition for Discharge** must be filed with the probate court.

This petition requests the court to release the personal representative (executor) from their duties, indicating that the estate has been fully administered.

Petition for Discharge Template

Note: This template is for illustrative purposes. Requirements may vary by jurisdiction, so it's essential to consult local court rules or an LDP or estate attorney.

[Your Name]
[Your Address]
[City, State, ZIP Code]
[Phone Number]
[Email Address]

[Date]

[Probate Court Name]
[Court Address]
[City, State, ZIP Code]

Re: Estate of [Deceased's Full Name], Deceased
Case No.: [Case Number]

Petition for Discharge of Personal Representative

Petitioner: [Your Full Name], Personal Representative of the Estate of [Deceased's Full Name].

1. Introduction:

Petitioner was appointed as the Personal Representative of the Estate of [Deceased's Full Name] on [Date of Appointment].

2. Administration of the Estate:

Petitioner has completed the administration of the estate as follows:

- **Asset Distribution:** All assets have been distributed to the rightful beneficiaries as per the [Will/Intestacy laws].

- **Debts and Taxes:** All known debts, claims, and taxes have been paid or settled.

- **Final Accounting:** A final accounting has been completed and is either filed with the court or waived by all beneficiaries.

3. Waivers and Consents:

Attached are waivers and consents from all beneficiaries acknowledging:

- Receipt of their respective distributions.

- Approval of the final accounting.

- Consent to the discharge of the Personal Representative.

4. Request for Discharge:

Petitioner respectfully requests that the Court:

- Approve this Petition for Discharge.

- Release Petitioner from all duties and liabilities as Personal Representative.

- Issue any further orders deemed appropriate.

5. Verification:

I declare under penalty of perjury under the laws of the State of [State] that the foregoing is true and correct.

[Your Signature]
[Your Typed Name]
Personal Representative of the Estate of [Deceased's Full Name]

Attachments:

- Waivers and Consents from Beneficiaries

- Final Accounting (if not waived)

Important Considerations

- **Jurisdictional Variations:** Procedures and requirements for filing a Petition for Discharge vary by state and county. It's crucial to consult your local probate court's rules or seek legal advice to ensure compliance.

- **Court Forms:** Some jurisdictions provide standardized forms for the Petition for Discharge. For example, California uses Form DE-295 for this purpose.
selfhelp.courts.ca.gov

- **Supporting Documents:** Ensure all necessary documents, such as waivers, consents, and final accountings, are prepared and attached as required by your jurisdiction.

By following the appropriate procedures and utilizing available resources, you can effectively petition for discharge and conclude the probate process.

Small Estate Thresholds & Simplified Probate

Each state sets a **small estate limit** that determines whether probate can be bypassed or simplified.

Examples:

- **California**: $184,500 limit (affidavit process available).

- **Texas**: $75,000 limit (small estate affidavit may be used).

- **Arizona**: $100,000 for real property; $75,000 for personal property.

If the estate qualifies for **small estate procedures**, you may be able to submit an affidavit instead of undergoing full probate.

Practical Tips for Avoiding Unnecessary Costs

- **Use a Small Estate Affidavit** if the estate qualifies to avoid full probate.

- **Minimize Attorney Fees** by handling simple probate tasks yourself.

- **Consult a Legal Document Preparer (LDP)** for document assistance instead of hiring an attorney.

- **Maintain Good Records** to prevent disputes and expedite the probate process.

- **Save on Costs**: Handle straightforward estates yourself to minimize attorney fees.

Conclusion

Probate can be a complex process, but with the right knowledge and preparation, you can navigate it effectively. Understanding your state's probate requirements, gathering necessary documents, and following the proper procedures will help ensure a smooth settlement of your loved one's estate.

The next chapter will cover **managing real estate** within an estate or trust, including transferring ownership, selling property, and handling mortgages and taxes.

Chapter 11
Managing Real Estate

Real estate is often one of the most significant assets in an estate or trust, making its proper management essential. As an **Executor** or **Trustee**, you will need to determine whether to sell or retain the property, address any mortgages or tax obligations, and ensure a smooth transition of ownership to beneficiaries.

This chapter will guide you through key steps for managing real estate within an estate or trust, covering legal requirements, financial considerations, and best practices for ensuring compliance with probate and trust administration laws.

We'll also cover tips when deciding whether to sell or retain the property, addressing mortgages and taxes, and preparing the property for sale if needed.

Assessing the Property's Status

Before making any decisions, gather the following information:

- **Ownership Documentation** – Locate the property deed to confirm ownership and determine whether it is held in the deceased's name or in a trust.

- **Mortgage and Liens** – Identify any outstanding mortgage balances, home equity loans, or tax liens.

- **Insurance Coverage** – Ensure the property remains insured during the administration period to protect against loss or liability.

- **Property Value** – Obtain a professional appraisal or comparative market analysis to determine the property's fair market value.

- **Beneficiary Preferences** – Discuss with beneficiaries whether they wish to retain or sell the property.

- **Financial Viability** – Evaluate whether the estate or trust has the financial resources to maintain the property (e.g., covering property taxes, mortgage payments, maintenance costs).

If the property is held **inside a trust**, the **Trustee** will have the authority to manage and transfer ownership. If the property is held **outside a trust**, the **Executor** must go through probate to legally transfer it.

Deciding Whether to Sell or Retain the Property

Factors to Consider:

1. **Financial Feasibility**:

   o   Assess the trust's or estate's financial position. Can the property be retained while meeting other obligations such as debts, taxes, or distributions to beneficiaries?

2. **Beneficiary Preferences**:

   o   Consult with beneficiaries. Do they wish to keep the property or prefer it be sold and the proceeds distributed?

3. **Legal Requirements**:

   o   Review the trust document or Will. Does it specify what should happen to the property?

   o   Ensure compliance with any restrictions or directives outlined in the governing documents.

4. **Property Costs**:

   o   Consider ongoing expenses such as mortgage pay-
       ments, insurance, property taxes, and maintenance.

5. **Market Conditions**:   `

   o   Evaluate current real estate market trends. Would
       selling the property now maximize its value?

Once you have gathered the necessary details, the next step is to
decide whether to sell or retain the property.

Reasons to Sell the Property

- The estate or trust lacks sufficient funds to maintain the
  property.

- The beneficiaries prefer a cash distribution rather than retaining real estate.

- The property is a secondary home or investment property
  that is difficult to manage.

- The property requires significant repairs or maintenance that are not financially feasible.

Reasons to Retain the Property

- A beneficiary wishes to live in or manage the property.

- The property is a family home with sentimental value.

- The property generates rental income that benefits the estate or trust.

- The real estate market conditions suggest appreciation in value.

Regardless of the decision, all actions should align with the wishes outlined in the **Will** or **Trust** and comply with state probate laws.

Handling Mortgages, Property Taxes, and Liens

If the property has a mortgage or outstanding debts, these must be addressed before transferring ownership or distributing proceeds.

1. Mortgage:

- **Determine Responsibility**: Verify whether the trust or estate is responsible for continuing mortgage payments.

- **Contact the Lender**: Notify the lender of the owner's death. Provide required documentation, such as the death certificate and proof of your role as trustee or executor.

- Request a **mortgage payoff statement** to determine the remaining balance.

Resolve Outstanding Balances:

- o If the property will be sold, ensure the mortgage is paid off at closing.

- o Check the county recorder's office for any outstanding liens (e.g., unpaid debts, judgments, tax liens).

- o Negotiate lien settlements or pay off debts before finalizing a sale or transfer.

o   If the property is retained, arrange for continued payments from the trust or estate account to avoid foreclosure.

2. Property Taxes:

- Check for unpaid property taxes and ensure they are settled to avoid penalties or liens.

- Confirm whether the trust or estate qualifies for any exemptions or reductions in property taxes.

- Pay past-due amounts before transferring ownership or selling the property.

3. Homeowners Insurance:

- Maintain or update insurance coverage to protect the property during the administration process.

- Inform the insurance company of the owner's death and update the policyholder information as needed.

4. Utilities and Maintenance:

- Keep utilities active to maintain the property's condition.

- Arrange for regular maintenance, such as landscaping or repairs, to preserve its value.

Preparing the Property for Sale

If selling the property is the best course of action, follow these steps to prepare it for sale:

1. **Secure the Property**:

   o Change the locks if necessary to prevent unauthorized access.

   o Remove personal items and valuables.

   o Maintain utility services (electricity, water, etc.) to preserve the property.

   o Keep homeowners insurance active until the sale is finalized.

2. **Address Repairs and Upgrades**:

    o   Complete necessary repairs to ensure the property is in good condition.

    o   Consider minor upgrades (e.g., painting, landscaping) to increase its market appeal.

3. **Obtain Necessary Court Approvals (If Applicable)**

    o   If probate is involved, the sale may require court approval.

    o   Some states require a **Notice of Proposed Action** to be sent to beneficiaries before selling estate property.

    o   Check with your probate attorney or court to confirm requirements.

4.   **Hire Professionals**:

   o   **Real Estate Agent**: Engage a local agent experienced in selling similar properties. They can provide a market analysis and help set the right price.

   o   **Appraiser**: Obtain a professional appraisal to establish the property's value.

   o   **Home Inspector**: Conduct an inspection to identify and address potential issues before listing.

3.   **Set the Listing Price**:

   o   Work with your real estate agent to set a competitive price based on market conditions and the property's appraised value.

5.   **Market the Property**:

   o   Use multiple channels to advertise the property, including online listings, open houses, and local print media.

6. **Review Offers**:

   o   Evaluate offers with the help of your real estate agent. Consider price, contingencies, and the buyer's financing.

7. **Close the Sale**:

   o   Work with a title company or attorney to handle the closing process.

   o   Ensure that proceeds are deposited into the trust or estate account.

Steps to Transfer Ownership to Beneficiaries

If the property is being transferred to beneficiaries, follow these steps:

1. Confirm Ownership & Legal Authority

- **If in a Trust:** The **Trustee** can transfer the property directly to the beneficiary by executing a new deed.

- **If in Probate:** The **Executor** must wait for court approval before transferring the deed to the beneficiary.

2. Prepare a New Deed

- Execute a **Grant Deed** or **Quitclaim Deed** to transfer ownership from the trust or estate to the beneficiary.

- Ensure the deed is notarized and signed by the **Trustee** or **Executor**.

3. Record the Deed

- The new deed must be recorded with the **county recorder's office** where the property is located.

- To find the appropriate office, search **"[County Name] Recorder's Office"** online.

- Pay the applicable recording fee (varies by state and county).

4. Update Property Tax & Insurance Records

- Notify the county tax assessor's office of the ownership change to update tax records.

- Ensure the new owner updates homeowners insurance coverage.

Practical Considerations for Executors and Trustees

- **Keep Beneficiaries Informed** – Maintain transparency with heirs regarding decisions related to the property.

- **Consult a Real Estate Attorney if Needed** – Certain transactions, especially in probate, may require legal guidance.

- **Document All Actions** – Keep records of communications, transactions, and property-related decisions for accountability.

- **Plan for Capital Gains Tax** – If the property is sold, understand tax implications, including the **step-up in basis** rule, which may reduce capital gains tax liability for heirs.

Conclusion

Managing real estate within an estate or trust requires careful planning and legal compliance. Whether transferring ownership to beneficiaries or selling the property, understanding the legal, financial, and logistical aspects ensures a smooth and efficient process.

In the next chapter, we will discuss **how to settle remaining debts and taxes** before finalizing distributions to beneficiaries.

Chapter 12
Distribute Remaining Assets

If you are serving as an **Executor** (managing assets through probate) or a **Trustee** (handling assets in a trust), your duty is to ensure all distributions align with legal requirements and the decedent's wishes.

This chapter provides a clear step-by-step guide for Executors and Trustees to properly distribute funds, real estate, and personal property while keeping records to protect against disputes.

Executor vs. Trustee: Who Handles What?

Before proceeding, determine whether you are acting as an Executor, a Trustee, or both:

- **Executor:** Handles assets that were owned **outside of a trust** and must be distributed through probate.

- **Trustee:** Manages assets held **within a trust** and follows the instructions outlined in the trust document.

If both roles exist in the estate, the **Executor and Trustee must coordinate** to ensure a smooth transition of assets.

Final Distribution Process

Step 1: Review the Estate Plan and Legal Documents

- If you are the **Executor**, carefully review the **Will** and court-approved inventory of probate assets.

- If you are the **Trustee**, thoroughly read the **trust document** to understand specific distribution instructions.

- Check for any conditions or timelines that affect distribution (e.g., age restrictions for beneficiaries, staggered payments, or special needs provisions).

Step 2: Ensure All Debts and Taxes Are Paid

Before distributing assets:

- **Executors** must ensure all valid debts, taxes, and probate fees are settled **before distributing probate assets**.

- **Trustees** must confirm that any outstanding trust-related expenses are resolved.

- **Both Executors and Trustees** should retain records of payments to creditors and tax authorities for final accounting purposes.

Skipping this step can result in personal liability if outstanding debts later surface.

Step 3: Prepare the Final Accounting

The final accounting summarizes all transactions related to the estate or trust. It should include:

- A list of all income received (e.g., rental income, investment gains).

- A breakdown of all expenses paid (e.g., debts, funeral costs, taxes).

- A schedule of remaining assets for distribution.

Some states require Executors to file the final accounting with the **probate court** before distributing assets.

Trustees, depending on state laws, may need to provide beneficiaries with an informal or formal final accounting.

Step 4: Obtain Beneficiary Releases

To protect yourself from future legal claims:

- Have each beneficiary **sign a release form** acknowledging receipt of their inheritance and waiving future claims against the estate or trust.

- Executors handling probate assets should retain these signed releases as part of the court's required documentation.

- Trustees should keep these records for personal protection and future reference.

Step 5: Distribute Assets According to the Will or Trust

1. Distributing Cash Assets

- **Executors:** Issue checks or wire transfers from the estate's bank account after court approval.

- **Trustees:** Transfer funds directly from the trust's account to beneficiaries.

- Record all transactions and obtain signed receipts.

Transferring Personal Property (Vehicles, Boats, Jewelry, Etc.)

If the deceased owned vehicles, motorcycles, boats, or other titled property, follow these steps:

Executors:

- o Verify whether the asset is listed in the Will or needs to be liquidated.

- o If selling, obtain fair market value and deposit proceeds into the probate estate.

- o If transferring, sign over the title to the beneficiary and notify the DMV.

Trustees:

- o If the asset was in the trust, transfer the title directly to the named beneficiary.

- o If the title is missing, request a **duplicate title** from the DMV by providing:

  - ▪ A certified death certificate.

  - ▪ A copy of the trust or Will (if applicable).

- Legal proof of authority (Letters Testamentary for Executors or Certification of Trust for Trustees).

Vehicles

Vehicles and similar items owned by the deceased require specific steps to transfer or sell. Here's how to handle them effectively:

1. Locate the Titles

- Check the deceased's personal files, safe deposit boxes, or records for original titles.

- If the title cannot be found:

    o Contact the state's Department of Motor Vehicles (DMV) or equivalent office to request a replacement title.

Provide documentation such as:

- A certified death certificate.

- Proof of your role as trustee or personal representative (e.g., Certificate of Trust in Existence and Authority).

- Any additional forms required by the DMV.

2. Transfer Ownership to Beneficiaries

- If the trust specifies a beneficiary for a vehicle, transfer the title to their name.

- Complete the transfer process at the DMV, which may require:

  - A Bill of Sale or Gift Affidavit (depending on the state).

  - Payment of applicable fees or taxes.

3. Sell the Vehicle (if not retained)

Prepare the Vehicle for Sale:

  - Ensure the vehicle is clean and in working condition.

  - Gather maintenance records or service history, if available.

Determine the Value:

  - Use tools like Kelley Blue Book or Edmunds to estimate the vehicle's fair market value.

Advertise the Sale:

- o List the vehicle on online marketplaces, local classi-fieds, or through a dealership.

Complete the Sale:

- o Draft a Bill of Sale.

- o Collect payment and ensure it is deposited into the trust account.

- o Sign over the title to the buyer.

- o Notify the DMV of the sale to release liability.

Step 6: Handle Special Distribution Cases

Certain distributions require additional steps:

Minor Beneficiaries:

- o Funds may need to be held in a custodial account or trust until the minor reaches adulthood.

Beneficiaries with Special Needs:

- o Funds should be directed to a **Special Needs Trust** if one exists, to avoid affecting government benefits.

Charitable Donations:

- o If the Will or Trust includes charitable gifts, contact the organization for proper transfer instructions.

Step 7: File Final Paperwork & Close the Estate or Trust

Executors:

- o Submit a **final accounting** to the probate court (if required).

- o File a **Petition for Discharge** to officially close the estate.

- o Distribute remaining funds and close the estate's bank account.

Trustees:

o   Issue a **final distribution statement** to all beneficiaries.

o   Retain records of all transactions in case of future inquiries.

o   Once all assets are distributed, close the trust's bank account.

Sample Petition for Discharge (For Executors)

[Executor's Name]
[Executor's Address]
[City, State, ZIP Code]
[Date]

[Probate Court Name]
[Court Address]
[City, State, ZIP Code]

Re: Estate of [Deceased's Name], Case No. [Case Number]

Petition for Discharge of Personal Representative

I, [Executor's Name], the duly appointed Executor/Administrator of the estate of [Deceased's Name], declare:

1. All assets have been distributed according to the Will/intestacy laws.
2. All debts, taxes, and claims have been settled.
3. Final accounting has been completed and approved.
4. I request discharge from my duties and formal closure of the estate.

Signed: [Executor's Name]
Dated: [Date]

Practical Tips for Distributing Assets

1. **Communicate Clearly**:

    o   Keep beneficiaries informed throughout the distribution process. Transparency reduces the risk of disputes.

    o   **Personal Property**: Distribute items directly to beneficiaries as specified in the trust.

2. **Document Everything**:

    o   Maintain records of all communications, distributions, and receipts for future reference.

    o   Keep a certified copy of the recorded deed for your records and provide one to the beneficiary.

3. **Seek Professional Help if Needed**:

    o   Engage a real estate attorney for property transfers or a tax professional for final tax filings.

4. **Address Disputes Quickly**:

    o   If beneficiaries disagree over distributions, mediate the issue promptly to avoid legal conflicts.

Final Thoughts

Whether you are serving as an **Executor** settling an estate through probate or a **Trustee** handling trust distributions, following the correct procedures ensures compliance and protects against disputes.

- **Executors:** Follow the court-supervised process to finalize and close the estate.

- **Trustees:** Carry out trust distributions according to the trust document's instructions.

- **Both should maintain meticulous records** and seek professional advice if needed.

The next and final chapter will guide you through **closing the estate or trust entirely**, ensuring all legal obligations are met and your role is officially completed.

Chapter 13
Close the Trust

The final step in trust administration is formally closing the trust. This process ensures that all tasks have been completed, all debts and taxes paid, and all assets distributed in accordance with the trust's instructions.

Closing the trust also protects the trustee by providing clear documentation of their actions.

Whether you are acting as an **Executor** (managing probate assets) or a **Trustee** (administering a trust), this chapter will guide you through the steps to close a trust, provide templates, and include a comprehensive checklist.

Executor vs. Trustee: Key Differences in Closing Procedures

- **Executors**: Must follow court procedures to finalize the estate, including submitting a **Petition for Discharge** and obtaining court approval before being released from responsibilities.

- **Trustees**: Must ensure all assets have been distributed, final tax returns filed, and records maintained before formally closing the trust.

If both roles exist in the estate, the **Executor and Trustee should coordinate** to ensure a smooth transition of assets and responsibilities.

Steps to Close the Trust

Step 1: Complete the Final Accounting

Before closing the estate or trust, a **final accounting** should be prepared. This document details all financial transactions, including: Prepare a detailed report summarizing all transactions during the trust administration, including:

- **Income received** (e.g., rental income, investment earnings, dividends).

- **Expenses paid** (e.g., debts, taxes, professional fees, trust or estate administration costs).

- **Distributions made** to beneficiaries.

- **Remaining balance** in the trust or estate (if applicable).

Executor's Responsibility

- Submit the final accounting to the **probate court** (if required by state law).

- Obtain **court approval** before making final distributions.

- Provide beneficiaries with a copy of the final accounting if necessary.

Trustee's Responsibility

- Provide an **informal** or **formal** final accounting to beneficiaries (depending on state requirements and trust terms).

- Ensure all distributions are documented and agreed upon by beneficiaries.

Step 2: Obtain Beneficiary Releases

To protect yourself from future legal claims, obtain a **signed release form** from each beneficiary acknowledging:

- Receipt of their distributions.

- Approval of the final accounting.

o   Release of the trustee from further liability.

Executor's Responsibility

- File beneficiary releases with the probate court if required.

Trustee's Responsibility

- Retain beneficiary releases for your records as proof of final distribution.

Use the template provided for a beneficiary release.

Beneficiary Release Template

[Your Name]
Trustee of [Name of Trust]
[Your Address]
[City, State, ZIP Code]
[Date]

Acknowledgment and Release by Beneficiary

I, [Beneficiary's Full Name], acknowledge receipt of my full distribution from the [Name of Trust], dated [Date of Trust]. I have reviewed the final accounting provided by the trustee and confirm the following:

1. I have received all assets to which I am entitled under the terms of the trust.

2. I approve the trustee's administration of the trust and the final accounting.

3. I release and discharge [Trustee's Name] from any and all claims, demands, or liabilities related to the administration of the trust.

Signed:
[Beneficiary's Signature]
Date: [Date]

Step 3: Distribute Any Remaining Funds

Before formally closing the trust or estate:

- **Executors**: Distribute any remaining probate assets **only after receiving court approval**.

- **Trustees**: Ensure all trust assets have been fully disbursed as per the trust's terms.

For **Executors**, final distributions may include:

- Final cash disbursements to heirs.

- Transferring real estate titles.

- Closing estate bank accounts.

For **Trustees**, final distributions may include:

- Completing any staggered or conditional payments.

- Ensuring real estate or titled assets have been properly transferred.

- Closing trust bank accounts.

Step 4: File Final Tax Returns

Before closing the trust or estate, make sure to:

- File the decedent's final personal income tax return (Form 1040).

- File an estate or trust tax return (Form 1041) if required.

- Pay any remaining taxes owed by the estate or trust.

If there is uncertainty about tax obligations, consult a CPA or tax professional to avoid penalties.

Step 5: Petition the Court to Close the Estate (For Executors Only)

Executors must file a **Petition for Discharge** with the probate court to formally close the estate. Once approved, the court will release the Executor from all duties.

Petition for Discharge Template (For Executors):

[Executor's Name]
[Executor's Address]
[City, State, ZIP Code]
[Date]

[Probate Court Name]
[Court Address]
[City, State, ZIP Code]

Re: Estate of [Deceased's Name], Case No. [Case Number]

Petition for Discharge of Personal Representative

I, [Executor's Name], the duly appointed Executor/Administrator of the estate of [Deceased's Name], declare:

1. All assets have been distributed according to the Will/intestacy laws.
2. All debts, taxes, and claims have been settled.
3. Final accounting has been completed and approved.
4. I request discharge from my duties and formal closure of the estate.

Signed: [Executor's Name]
Dated: [Date]

Step 6: Declare the Trust Closed (For Trustees Only)

For Trustees, once all assets are distributed and final accounting is complete, issue a **Declaration of Trust Closure** to formally close the trust.

Declaration of Trust Closure Template

Sample Declaration of Trust Closure (For Trustees):

I, [Your Full Name], as trustee of the [Name of Trust], declare the following:

1.   All assets of the trust have been distributed in accordance with the trust's terms.

2.   All debts, taxes, and administrative expenses have been paid.

3.   The trust's final income tax return has been filed, and any taxes owed have been paid.

4.   The trust bank account has been closed.

5.   The trust is now fully administered and formally closed.

Signed:
[Your Signature]
Date: [Date]

Step 7: Retain Records

Even after the trust or estate is closed, **keep copies of all relevant documents for at least 5-7 years**, including:

- Final accounting reports.

- Beneficiary releases.

- Tax filings and proof of payments.

- Court documents (if probate was required).

This ensures protection in case of future disputes or audits.

Closing the Trust Checklist

Use this checklist to ensure all steps are completed:

1. Final Accounting

2. Beneficiary Releases

3. Distribute Remaining Funds

4. Final Tax Returns

5. Declaration of Trust Closure

6. Retain Records

Final Thoughts

Whether you are an **Executor finalizing an estate** through probate or a **Trustee completing trust administration**, following these steps will ensure all legal and financial obligations are met.

- **Executors** must obtain court approval before formally closing the estate.

- **Trustees** can close the trust once all distributions and tax obligations are completed.

- **Both roles require careful documentation** to avoid future liability.

By completing this final step, you **officially conclude your responsibilities** and bring closure to the administration process, ensuring that your loved one's wishes have been carried out successfully.

This concludes the guide. If you've made it this far, congratulations—you have successfully navigated one of the most complex responsibilities in estate and trust administration!

Chapter 14
Wrapping It All Up

Congratulations! If you've reached this chapter, take a deep breath —you have successfully navigated one of the most complex responsibilities in estate and trust administration.

Whether you stepped into the role as an **Executor**, managing the probate process and distributing estate assets, or as a **Trustee**, overseeing a trust's administration and ensuring beneficiaries receive their inheritances, you've done something truly meaningful.

This journey is filled with legal complexities, emotional weight, and financial decisions, but by following the steps laid out in this guide, you have honored your loved one's wishes and provided a smooth transition for the beneficiaries.

A Look Back at the Journey

Throughout this book, we've covered every major step of this process. Here's a recap of the major milestones you've accomplished:

1. Understanding Your Role

You took the time to learn what it means to be an Executor or Trustee, understanding your fiduciary duties and responsibilities to beneficiaries and creditors alike. Recognizing the difference between these roles helped you determine the correct legal steps and procedures to follow.

2. Gathering and Organizing Documents

You located and reviewed the Will, trust documents, financial statements, property deeds, and legal filings. This foundation ensured a seamless administration process and prevented unnecessary delays or disputes.

3. Notifying Creditors and Beneficiaries

You insured that all beneficiaries were properly notified about their interests in the estate or trust in a timely manner to prevent legal complications and ensure transparency. You also notified creditors to start the legal timeframe within which they must submit claims, ultimately protecting the estate or trust from future liability.

4. Consulting Professionals When Needed

Whether through a brief consultation with an estate attorney, tax professional, or Legal Document Preparer (LDP), you leveraged expert insights when necessary—saving thousands in legal fees while still ensuring compliance.

5. Managing Assets and Debts

You secured and protected real estate, bank accounts, retirement funds, and personal property. You also properly identified and handled creditors, ensuring that valid debts were paid while protecting the estate or trust from illegitimate claims.

6. Navigating Probate (If Required)

As an **Executor**, you may have filed probate paperwork, attended hearings, and followed court-mandated steps to distribute assets in accordance with the Will or state intestacy laws.

7. Administering a Trust (If Applicable)

As a **Trustee**, you upheld the terms of the trust, managed assets, handled tax filings, and ensured beneficiaries received their rightful inheritance in accordance with the trust document.

8. Distributing Assets to Beneficiaries

You carefully followed the trust's or Will's instructions for distributing cash, real estate, personal property, and other assets—ensuring all legal steps were followed and documentation was properly maintained.

9. Filing Taxes and Closing the Trust or Estate

From obtaining a Tax ID (EIN) to filing the decedent's final tax return, you made sure that tax obligations were met. You also completed the final accounting, secured beneficiary releases, and legally closed the estate or trust.

Final Thoughts: Lessons Learned

1. Organization and Documentation Are Key

Whether acting as an **Executor** or **Trustee**, keeping clear records of transactions, communications, and legal filings protected you from liability and made the process smoother.

2. Patience and Persistence Pay Off

Administering an estate or trust is not an overnight process. Some steps may have taken longer than expected, but your diligence ensured a proper and legally sound administration.

3. Saving Money Doesn't Mean Cutting Corners

By learning the process and handling much of the work yourself, you potentially saved thousands of dollars in attorney fees. But when necessary, you sought professional help—striking the right balance between DIY administration and expert guidance.

4. You Honored Your Loved One's Wishes

Beyond the legal and financial aspects, you fulfilled an important role in carrying out your loved one's final wishes. This is a responsibility that many find daunting, but you stepped up and completed it with care and dedication.

A Few Words of Encouragement

Taking on the role of an Executor or trustee can feel overwhelming at times, but remember: you are not alone. Resources like this guide, supportive professionals, and tools like legal document preparers and ChatGPT are here to help.

You are honoring someone's legacy by ensuring their wishes are carried out and their loved ones are cared for. That is no small accomplishment, and it reflects your dedication and care.

Your Next Steps

As you conclude your role, take a moment to reflect on what you've achieved. Managing the probate process and distributing estate assets or administering a trust is not just about following legal requirements; it's about ensuring that the deceased's final wishes are respected. If challenges arise in the future, remember the knowledge and skills you've gained through this process.

Finally, consider sharing your experience. Others in your position could benefit from your insights and encouragement. Whether it's guiding a family member or sharing tips with a friend, your journey can inspire and help others navigate this responsibility.

Thank You for Trusting This Guide

Thank you for allowing this guide to be part of your journey. It was created with the goal of making a complex process easier to understand and empowering you to take control of this process with confidence.

I hope it has empowered you to take control of the situation, save unnecessary legal costs, and, most importantly, bring closure to this chapter with clarity and peace of mind.

Should you face a similar role in the future, you now have a strong foundation to build upon.

You have successfully completed your role as an **Executor or Trustee**. Now, it's time to move forward with confidence, knowing that you did everything in your power to honor your loved one's legacy.

Congratulations on a job well done!

Need more help or updates?

Follow us on Instagram for bite-sized tips, video walkthroughs, and free content to guide you through every stage of estate settlement.

Our Instagram is: **@SettleAnEstate**

www.ingramcontent.com/pod-product-compliance
Lightning Source LLC
Chambersburg PA
CBHW031501120626
46545CB00005B/1695